How to run a pressure group

D1784847

ALDINE PAPERBACKS

Aldine Paperbacks embrace a wide range of interests, from Dylan Thomas's *Under Milk Wood* and *Collected Poems* to Mary Norton's *The Borrowers* stories, and cover Art, Literature, Social Questions, Cookery, Games and Sport, Gardening etc. A complete list is available from booksellers or the publishers on request.

Christopher Hall

How to run
a pressure group

J M Dent & Sons Ltd   London

First published 1974
© Christopher Hall 1974

Made in Great Britain by
The Aldine Press · Letchworth · Herts
for J. M. Dent & Sons Ltd
Aldine House · Albemarle Street · London

This book is set in 10 point Times New Roman

ISBN: 0 460 02143 5

Contents

Acknowledgment

My thanks are due to the Civic Trust for permission to reproduce the model constitution for civic societies (Appendix B).

Introduction

Pressure groups are a well-established feature of public life in this country. One of the first and most successful was the Anti-Corn Law League, whose triumph in 1846 shattered the pattern of politics for a generation.

Trade unions, local authority associations, charitable bodies concerned with the welfare of children, the disabled and the poor, the National Farmers' Union, the Council for the Protection of Rural England, the A.A. and the R.A.C., the British Roads Federation and the Pedestrians' Association for Road Safety—all these are pressure groups at least some of the time and part of their working lives. All of them seek to influence the policy of central or local government in a direction favourable to their members and interests.

This book is written for a newer phenomenon, the local pressure group, and especially for those local pressure groups which spring up to deal with some sudden crisis in the affairs of a community. Such groups have increasingly come to be accepted in recent years as having a role in the processes of consultation which lead to official decisions. The force of their opposition to some notorious official proposals has been recogn'zed. But such groups still have a long way to go before they achieve the solid recognition extended to their national pressure group colleagues.

There are great and damaging inequalities between local pressure groups. The spectacular success of a few groups misleads people into supposing that the position of the *ad hoc* pressure group is now secure. The most notable such success was the victory of the Wing Airport Resistance Association which in 1971 prevented London's Third Airport being sited at Cublington in Buckinghamshire. But W.A.R.A. represented an affluent middle-class constituency (though at times it did its best to disguise itself as a bunch of tractor-driving yokels). It was never short of money or unpaid professional advice.

It fought a selfish campaign. It did not merely say 'No Wings over Wing' (the campaign slogan); it pressed for the airport to be sited on Foulness where the few hundred inhabitants were mostly old age pensioners and powerless to mount an effective reply.

One object of this book is to show those who need a pressure group of their own how to run one. They cannot all be equipped with the money to hire public relations consultants, but they can be taught simple publicity techniques which will serve them as well as any PR outfit can. They cannot all command a membership rich in planners, architects, company directors and other practised manipulators of government. But they can be told where to go to get advice and how to maximize the force of their own arguments.

Of course this information and these techniques will be used by bad guys as well as good. They can be used equally by innocent men of good will seeking to save an historic street from destruction, or by racialists trying to prevent black families being housed on their estate.

It is in the nature of democracy that this should be so. What matters is that the voices should be equal and that the built-in advantages of wealth and position should be minimized. If we believe in democracy we must believe in the ability of ordinary people, through their representatives, to choose the right more often than the wrong.

Those who dislike the idea of equality of voices will sneer at much of this book, because what it says will be—to them— very simple and very obvious. What I have tried to do is to write down what anyone starting a local pressure group may need to know or find out.

People who habitually influence opinion will find it all old hat. Those who don't make a habit of it, but for whom it may some time or other be a necessity, will I hope find it useful.

March 1973   Christopher Hall

1
How to start

It is hard to believe that there is any kind of issue anywhere which cannot be dealt with through an existing voluntary organization. If your green belt is threatened there is a county branch of the Council for the Protection of Rural England; if the council plans a disastrous new inner ring road there will be a civic society or residents' association or Friends of Old Muddlecombe; if you are concerned about the local schools, why form a new body when you could start a branch of the National Association for the Advancement of State Education?

You may be lucky. It may be that the existing organizations will cope satisfactorily. But often it is not so. And this is not because the existing organizations are no good. It is because the nature of pressure groups is that they derive their impetus and strength from the immediacy of their problems. In the South End Green area of Camden local people were faced a few years ago with a plan by the borough council to widen a railway bridge in a shopping and residential area into a four-lane road. This was the first step towards widening a further stretch of road which would then carve into Hampstead Heath.

The local residents could have made their objections to this scheme through an existing local protection society. And they could have worked through such national bodies as the Pedes-trians' Association for Road Safety and the Commons, Open Spaces and Footpaths Preservation Society to defeat the scheme.

They preferred to set up a new local civic group to deal with this one problem, and drawing its membership only from the neighbourhood directly affected. They were right to do this because people are always readier to join an organization

9

catering for a clearly local need, and which carries no dead-weight of other aims and ideas in which they are not interested. And by creating a specialist organization they ensured that their officers and committee concentrated only on the issue of the moment.

This particular group also illustrates the classic method by which permanent local pressure groups are formed. The problem of the road-widening which had called the organization into being was dealt with (successfully) in a matter of eighteen months. The society, however, remained in being and has since served to focus local opinion on a number of environmental issues and to keep a standing watchdog role over developments in the neighbourhood.

Hampstead is not exceptional. There are scores of towns and villages throughout the country where a stranger with an orderly mind would be surprised at the multiplicity of environmental and preservation groups. It is nothing unusual to have two amenity societies operating in the same territory. In Somerset, for example, the Friends of the Quantocks look after that miniature and lovely line of hills, although the Somerset branch of the Council for the Protection of Rural England includes the area within its remit. The small town of Tring in Hertfordshire has two local organizations concerned with the town's development—the Ratepayers' Association and the Tring Society—while the Hertfordshire Society (the local CPRE branch) and the Chiltern Society both deal with amenity problems in the neighbourhood.

From time to time people appear on the amenity scene who wring their hands at this amoeba-like proliferation of societies. 'Why don't they get together and form a single organization, or federate in some way?' say these reformers. 'Surely they would be stronger if united?'

This is a fundamental misunderstanding of how local pressure groups work. The virtue of such organizations is that they represent a *local* point of view. Little Muddlecombe and Great Muddlecombe may have diametrically opposed views on the route of a new motorway, because one route will affect one village and an alternative the other. A federation of local societies would probably end up by limply refusing to take a firm line rather than upset one constituent organization. A single society covering both villages would split down the middle. Even if a single amenity society did manage to decide which village was to have the dirty end of the stick, why should it? These decisions are for Government to make and for Government to justify. The pressure group's job is to represent to Government the objections to a particular course of action.

This is not to say that a pressure group never has a constructive role to play in putting forward an alternative to official policy which commands general support in its constituency. But the lesson is that no individual or group of individuals should ever feel deterred from starting their own *ad hoc* organization unless they are quite certain that an existing body is fully capable of representing their views. The fact that a few people feel a special organization would be a good idea is enough to indicate that it will have a useful role to play.

Siren voices claiming that this is the road to anarchy will not be lacking. The bigger, longer established organization will claim a right to handle the issue. But the new boys, if they have a special case to put, will attract members. People are parochial. They will join a village, estate or even street defence organization when a town- or county-based society seems too remote. And they will go to endless pains to set up their own local show when volunteers to start and run a branch of something bigger will be lacking.

How to start

'Let's form a committee', is the traditional cry of the British citizen faced with a problem concerning more than himself alone. And it is usually the right thing to do. But a committee must be legitimized. It must be more than a few self-appointed persons. It must have a mandate visibly derived from as wide a body of people as possible. Otherwise the authorities will take no notice of it.

The method of achieving a mandate outlined below is the commonest and simplest way of going about it. It has the added advantage of being plainly democratic. It does not leave the committee open to any charge of being unrepresentative.

The foundation of this method is the well-publicized meeting which resolves to establish the organization and appoints a committee to get on with the job.

11

The launching meeting

There are three conditions of success for the launching meeting:
1. The premises must be right. 2. Enough people must be
informed long enough in advance. 3. The platform of speakers
and the Chairman must know exactly what is wanted from the
meeting and must be competent to achieve it.

Some guidelines

Choose a place which is central to the area from which your
supporters will be drawn and which is handy for public transport. Timing is important. If your organization aims to serve
a geographically nucleated community a week-day evening is
as good as any (but see the remarks about the best days of the
week for press coverage in Chapter 3, pages 32, 38). If your
centre is a country town and you seek support from the villages
around, a Saturday afternoon is likely to be best. A good rule
is to choose a hall rather too small for the numbers you hope
to attract. With any luck you will have people standing at the
back and sides, which creates a sense of enthusiasm and enables
the local press to headline their report: 'Protest Meeting
Packed Out'. A check list of detailed arrangements for a public
meeting is given in Appendix A.

Publicity for the meeting need not be sophisticated. One of
the most successful pressure groups I know started with one
man and his wife delivering a brief typed and duplicated notice
door to door. The cause was a rail closure, and without any
other publicity than that they packed the town hall.

If time and money permit I recommend use of a printed
handbill measuring about $5\frac{1}{2}$ by 8 inches. The advantage of
this size is that it can be used both as a notice to put through
letter-boxes and as a small poster for display in front windows
and on notice boards.

Printers' prices vary, but a small jobbing printer outside
London is likely to charge about £4 to £5 for 500 handbills of
this size, carrying the time and place of the meeting, the names
of a Chairman and three speakers plus a headline.

With time and volunteers in short supply, get your distribution priorities right. Think first of the places lots of people go
to or pass regularly: shops, works' notice boards, any public
notice boards in the vicinity, house windows at commanding

positions, the public library (they will usually display anything not too obviously political), pubs, cafés, dry-cleaners, launderettes and so on. Remember that fly-posting (sticking notices on other people's walls) is illegal but often done.

Only when you are sure you can cover these locations should you start house-to-house distribution. By definition a notice delivered to a house has on average less drawing power than one publicly displayed.

Last of all consider handing out notices to passers-by in some public place, for example, the local shopping centre. This is certainly not a waste of time, but the recipients are at their least receptive when any unwanted piece of paper is thrust into their hands.

There is no need to worry because your notice is a simple, perhaps crude, piece of work. If people are concerned about the issue it advertises they won't mind about that. There is even some psychological advantage in being seen to be doing the job on a shoe-string in order to get into action quickly.

For the same reason it is a mistake to give too much notice of the launching meeting. A week is about right in a closely knit community—two weeks if your catchment area is wider.

Platform and purpose
Publicizing the meeting successfully requires only that the organizers follow the simple rules given above. The tricky part is getting the meeting itself right and seeing that it achieves its purpose. A clear definition of that purpose in the minds of the organizers is essential.

The sort of groups we are considering usually start as protests, either against some official proposal (for instance, a new road, a clearance scheme, a rail closure, a rent increase) or against some official failure (for example, a local authority refusing concessionary fares to old age pensioners or failing to introduce comprehensive schools), or against some private scheme (for instance, a housing estate in the green belt or the destruction of an historic building). The element of protest is vital. The meeting must express that as vigorously and unanimously as possible. The other side must get the impression of instant, unanimous and numerous opposition.

The organizers of the meeting must know what machinery

13

they need to conduct the subsequent campaign. It is very unlikely that a single protest meeting will do the trick. The platform at the launching meeting must be carefully briefed on what is wanted and how to get it.

There is a modish view that true democracy demands 'unstructured' meetings, from which alone the true will of those present can emerge. Careful planning of the meeting's form and purpose will be condemned by those who take this view as undemocratic manipulation of the people. There are groups which can afford this attitude—students, for instance, for whom protest is a form of self-expression rather than a serious political activity or vital self-defence—though in practice 'unstructured' meetings usually fall prey to manipulation by an unscrupulous and well-organized faction.

It is not manipulation of anybody to provide an opportunity for organized protest and to channel that protest into a well-directed campaign. Manipulation only occurs if anyone attending the meetings is denied the right to put a contrary opinion, or if the organizers fraudulently claim a mandate which the meeting has refused them.

Those who sit on the platform and speak at the launching meeting must satisfy one *or more* of the following criteria:

1. They must be well known locally or nationally so that they can add weight to the cause and attract publicity for it.

2. They must be able to speak competently in public, and one at least should be an effective rabble-rouser, so that the maximum of emotional drive is generated.

3. They must be expert on the subject and have expert advice to give.

4. They must represent or be members of voluntary organizations or local authorities whose support the organizers want.

The Chairman is the most difficult choice of all. He must *not* be chosen simply because he is well known, well liked or respectable. He must be chosen because he is a skilful chairman and can bring the meeting to make the decisions the organizers want. If he is also respectable, well known locally or nationally famous, that is a bonus.

This is how the platform might look at the launching meeting

14

of an association formed to oppose the closure of a local railway line:

Chairman: Chairman of the local Conservative Association. Known for his skilful chairmanship because he recently handled a stormy meeting of the Association to choose the next election candidate. Obviously also a prominent local figure.

Speakers: i. A member of the Executive Committee of the National Council on Inland Transport, a national pressure group which has been fighting rail closures since the days of Dr Beeching. Chosen for expert advice on statutory procedures.
ii. Secretary of local Trades Council. Picked to balance the Chairman politically and show that this is an issue which transcends party boundaries. He is especially concerned because the closure will mean loss of jobs to his affiliated railway union branches.
iii. Prominent member of local federation of Women's Institutes. To give consumers' point of view and represent smaller settlements served by the line in countryside.

This is likely to be enough speakers for the platform. Which order you run them in does not matter very much. Notice that all the criteria listed have been fulfilled by one or more of the speakers except that none of these is a notable spell-binder. Any community will have people around who satisfy the other criteria just waiting to be used. The art of emotional public oratory is harder to find.

Failing an obvious candidate for the job, anyone who speaks effectively and with sincerity will do. He or she need not be billed to speak from the platform, because the organizers still have one vital slot to fill: the mover of the resolution calling for the establishment of a permanent organization. Never leave this to chance. The speaker and the precise form of words should be worked out beforehand. The moment is for the Chairman to decide, with his eye on the clock and his ear to the tempo and enthusiasm of the contributions from the floor which follow the platform speakers. As likely as not the best person to move the resolution will be the individual who first decided to call the meeting.

15

The name of the mover of this resolution and the text of the resolution can be given on the notice of the meeting or agenda available at the meeting. Marginally this is a disadvantage. It destroys any element of surprise about the meeting. A better audience response will be achieved if the Chairman lets the discussion run until people are beginning to say, 'What are we going to *do*?' than if they know down to the last detail what they will be asked to do. The discussion can be helped to move in the right direction if a few reliable people are invited to catch the Chairman's eye.

The first decision
The passing of the launching resolution is the first formal decision of the campaign. It governs everything that happens thereafter. Get it right. The resolution should be firm, quotable and comprehensive.

In the hypothetical example of an association formed to prevent a rail closure it might read like this: 'That this meeting of concerned citizens deplores the decision of British Rail to close the passenger service on the XY line; considers that this closure would lead not only to grave hardship to many members of the communities served by the line but also to added traffic congestion and increased inconvenience of various kinds; and therefore resolves to form an association which shall oppose the closure of the line.' This looks straightforward enough, but there are several things to note about it.

First, it is more than a statement of protest. It formally establishes the association for a specific purpose. This is important in case the mandate of the association and its committee is ever challenged. Secondly, it sets out in brief the reasons for opposing closure: hardship and other side-effects on the communities involved. This makes the resolution a valuable summing-up of the meeting for the benefit of the press.

The committee
All this began with a handful of individuals saying 'Form a committee', and with the resolution passed they can do just that. A pitfall here is to try to elect *officers* at this stage. To do so often saddles a new organization with the most vociferous

or locally best-known characters as its leaders when they may be quite unsuited to the job. You certainly do not want the Secretary of the Trades Council or the Chairman of the local NUR branch to head a railway defence association. Their 'vested interest' is too obvious. Nor do you want anyone from one of the local political groups, since it may put off those of the opposite persuasion. Still less do you want anyone who is already deeply committed to voluntary activity in some other field: he or she will not have time for a new organization. But these are the sort of people a mass meeting will elect because those present will go for a familiar face or name.

What you want in the key posts are the individuals who set the ball rolling—the ones who found time and enthusiasm for this particular cause in the first place. So the meeting should be asked simply to elect a steering committee which will choose its own officers. As soon as the resolution is passed the Chairman should say something like this: 'Ladies and gentlemen: it is getting late and I know that some of you have quite a long way to get home. We have transacted the principal business that we came here to deal with. We have expressed our opposition to this proposal in no uncertain manner. It remains for us to establish the machinery that will implement our purpose. I therefore propose that as the last business this evening we choose a steering committee which will have the task of launching our campaign and reporting to a further public meeting in a month's time.'

The Chairman then goes on to ask for nominations to the steering committee from the floor. Some at least of these should be obvious and others prearranged. If the Chairman is wise he will have asked for 'a dozen or so names', thus enabling himself to close nominations whenever he thinks he has the right balance, geographically, politically and socially. By the time the steering committee thus chosen meets, it will be well known who started things off. In any case the Chairman may have directed the matter by nominating the prime mover as convener of the steering committee. He will then be able to take his pick of the two key posts: Chairman and Secretary.

The last business of the evening is for the Chairman to ask the steering committee to remain behind to fix the time and place of their first meeting (preferably within a few days), and

17

to remind those attending to sign the attendance list before they leave if they have not already done so.

Alternative methods

There are two alternative methods of legitimizing a pressure campaign which are worth considering:

Federation   When a number of existing organizations unite for a particular purpose it may be sufficient for them to appoint a joint committee. There are several examples of this form of organization among amenity societies. Typical is the North Wales (Hydro-Electricity) Protection Committee, on which representatives of such bodies as the Council for the Protection of Rural Wales, the Ramblers' Association and the Youth Hostels Association all serve together. But even where there is such an obvious common purpose the organization is likely to lack drive unless some of its members are individuals wholly dedicated to the particular struggle.

Unstructured committee   It is not unknown for campaign committees to be entirely self-appointed. Such groups can derive an adequate mandate by holding regular public meetings at which they report back on their activities and obtain popular support for what they are doing.

Both these methods have their difficulties. In the first case members of the campaign committee may be inhibited from action by the need to obtain a mandate from their nominating body. In the second there is no mass membership paying a subscription and providing regular funds. Moreover the second type of committee would probably find itself subjected to severe questioning at a public inquiry or other form of tribunal about its claim to represent anyone but itself.

2
Personnel and jobs

The steering committee elected at the launching meeting has a lot to do. In a typical case it will be plunged immediately into a campaign apparently requiring all its attention and effort. But its members have also to provide a new organization with a constitution and rules. However temporary you think the organization may be, it should have basic rules. In fact, as we have seen, groups formed to deal with an apparently temporary situation often find themselves a permanent role later.

And there is also the problem of legitimacy. Unless the organization is properly constituted it leaves itself open to awkward questions by cross-examining counsel at a public inquiry or sneers in the local press from councillors whose policies it is opposing.

The steering committee elected at the launching meeting should report back to a second general meeting as soon as possible. A simple statement of policy should be approved at this meeting. A constitution should be adopted and the steering committee should become the executive committee by election from the general meeting in accordance with that constitution.

At Appendix B is the text of the model constitution for civic societies prepared by the Civic Trust. This obviously will not do for every type of organization but it should provide some ideas to be working on. It is so drawn that societies adopting it qualify for recognition as charities by the Charity Commissioners. The advantages and disadvantages of obtaining charitable status are discussed in Chapter 4.

To begin with, a very simple constitution will do. The essential points are:

1. The constitution begins by naming the organization and listing its aims. Draw these widely rather than narrowly. Situations develop. The hypothetical railway defence association of Chapter 1 may find itself tackling public transport generally before long.

2. Define the membership and powers of the central Executive Committee. Make sure that (a) it has power to co-opt new members (within reason); (b) it is clearly empowered by the constitution to act and speak in the name of the whole organization without continual reference to a general meeting; and (c) it can appoint sub-committees and settle their terms of reference.

3. Set a minimum frequency for EC meetings and an approximate date for the Annual General Meeting.

4. Provide for minimum notice of annual and other general meetings and make it possible for a given number of ordinary members to call a general meeting if they wish.

5. Arrangements for winding up the organization and disposing of its funds or assets should be included. If they are not, individuals can be left with a messy situation in which they don't know what to do for the best.

What the constitution should *not* include is the rate of membership subscription. Most constitutions, rightly, can only be amended by two-thirds majorities of a general meeting and this could seriously delay necessary changes in the subscription rate.

Committee and officers
Executive Committee   Whatever other structure the organization develops, this is the key to the whole thing. The EC will do the day-to-day work. It will make instant policy, either consciously or by the accretion of particular decisions; it will react to moves by the other side during a campaign. It will at all times manage the organization. Hence the importance of the powers outlined for it in the constitution.

Its size will depend on what sort of organization you are running. The more informal your proceedings the smaller the committee consistent with efficiency. If the EC has an efficient Secretary, properly written-up minutes and agenda circulated in advance, and an expeditious Chairman, as many as twenty people can function effectively as a committee. But if minutes are a chatty approximation to what occurred, which nobody sees before they get to the meeting, and the agenda is a scrap of paper that the Secretary wrote on while gobbling down his tea, then you will find a dozen members too many.

Officers You need, obviously, a Chairman, a Secretary and a Treasurer. And that is all you absolutely need, but there is a strong case for a Vice-chairman and an assistant or minutes secretary. A Vice-chairman is a useful stand-in both in the chair and as a spokesman if the Chairman happens to be away. An efficient shorthand-typist who can produce an accurate record of a meeting saves the overworked Secretary a very time-consuming chore. Small organizations can afford to leave the handling of membership to the Treasurer, but many will find it more effective to appoint a Membership Secretary whose job is to handle subscriptions, keep membership records and remind members when subs are due. This officer will also be responsible for activities aimed at recruiting new members.

Presidents and Vice-presidents There is no hurry about these. They are big names to grace your notepaper and occasionally a deputation. They can be collected at leisure. In some organizations the President is asked to take the chair at AGMs. This is fine if he is really in touch with what is going on and is an efficient chairman.

Council
This is the name given by a number of bodies to a second tier of authority lying between the EC and the general meeting. It is by no means essential to all pressure groups, but it is especially useful in those with a large affiliated membership among other organizations. For example a regional amenity society, as well as having several thousand individual members, may also have a hundred or so local preservation societies, local authorities and parish councils as affiliated (or corporate) members. A council meeting three or four times a year would aim primarily at providing a forum for these bodies at which the EC would report. The power granted to Council should be

21

carefully defined. There is no reason why it should not take general policy decisions. Indeed it is useful to have a body of opinion wider than the EC, but smaller than a general meeting, at which long-term policy ideas can be aired and refined. But the Council's powers must not be allowed to conflict with the EC's job of running the organization and making the day-to-day decisions.

Frequency of committees
There are no general rules, but the Executive Committee of a pressure group should normally meet at least once a month, even when things are quiet. Even a watchdog role cannot be performed adequately with less frequent meetings. During the run-up to a major public inquiry or the presentation to Parliament of a petition against a private Bill, weekly meetings may well be needed.

Meeting place
The EC's efficiency depends on this. Far too many committees meet in the living-room of one of their members. Everyone lounges comfortably in armchairs or perches on cushions. The Chairman is sunk so deep in the corner of the sofa that he can neither be heard nor tell who wishes to be heard. Private dialogues spring up in corners. The host member's wife interrupts to ask who wants their coffee black, and the serving of coffee further disrupts the business. The first rule of an effective committee is that its members sit up to a table on which they can put their papers and the Chairman sits at the end where he can see and hear everyone. The Secretary and the Treasurer sit on either side of him. Refreshments—if you must have them— should be got out of the way before the meeting or left until after. If no member can provide a room which meets these criteria then it is well worth hiring one. There will be no difficulty in finding a local pub which will let an upstairs room for at most a pound or so, and possibly for nothing, in the expectation of selling a few extra pints after the meeting.

If you think your group can do without these harsh formalities, remember: a properly run meeting gets through the business very much more quickly; there is no confusion about

what was decided or who is to do what. Everyone hears what
is said and has a chance to be heard. Pressure groups are usually
fighting professionals equipped with full Whitehall or local
government or big corporation paraphernalia of decision- and
policy-making. The members of a pressure group are amateurs,
and that means they have no time to waste. They have to beat
the professionals at the professionals' own game. Clear and
expeditious decision-making is fundamental.

Annual General Meeting

The AGM of a voluntary organization is one of the most sacred
rites of British democracy, and like most sacred rites is usually
dull and perfunctory.

The officers report haltingly on the year's work. The Treasurer points out that the interest on the society's minuscule
investments has produced £4.75 and that unless more members
are recruited the subscription will have to be raised. The annual
report and accounts are passed after a lifeless discussion (if
any), terminated by one of those useful characters who never
say anything else in public except 'Beg t'm've, Mr Chairman'.

With painful modesty the officers and committee allow their
names to go forward for re-election, with profuse protestations
of readiness to stand down for somebody else (unknown).
With luck two committee members will retire and two more
be press-ganged to take their place. The Chairman will blush-
ingly surrender the chair to someone else while his own re-
election is moved. But all will move heaven and earth to avoid
the embarrassment of a vote on any of the nominations.

The repetition of this sort of thing makes AGMs a bad joke.
Of course an AGM must conduct certain formal business, and
in a well-run organization whose officers carry the confidence
of the membership it is not necessary that there should be a
dog-fight for the chief offices each year. But the AGM is an
opportunity for the leadership of the organization to keep in
touch with the membership, and if the leadership is sensible
they will take it. It should not be the only opportunity. There
ought to be at least one other general meeting during the year,
and there should also be some printed communication with
members (see Chapter 3). The more that members are told what
their officers are doing the more likely they are to offer their

23

whole-hearted support. Secrecy and lack of communication breed at best apathy and at worst suspicion.

The annual report and accounts of even the smallest society should be circulated *in advance* of the AGM with the notice of meeting, or made available at the meeting in duplicated typescript or printed form. At the meeting the Chairman and Secretary should introduce the report, commenting on any items of special interest or developing ideas which are likely to be important for the next year's work. The Treasurer should do the same for the accounts. To keep formally within the rules of order a useful method is for the Chairman or Secretary to move adoption of the report and accounts and for the Treasurer to second.

This motion should never be taken as a formality. Time should always be allowed for debate and questions. If there are no queries from the floor it is a sign that the organization commands little interest or enthusiasm among its members. Members of the EC should speak to or answer questions on the points of the report they have been especially concerned with.

The other business which must be transacted at the AGM is the election of the EC and officers and Council if the organization has one. When drawing up the constitution resist any proposal for a system whereby only part of the committee retires each year. Contact between committees and members is usually so tenuous in even the best intentioned organizations that the least the leadership can do is submit itself to an annual vote of confidence.

Absence of interest in the elections indicates flagging interest in the organization. Gradual renewal of the leadership is essential to the health of the organization. However keen and dedicated voluntary officers may be, they cannot continue indefinitely without loss of energy and ideas. In a normally active organization three years is a sufficient spell for a Chairman or Secretary. A Treasurer, unless he is deeply involved in serious fund-raising, has a more routine job and can be left for longer. For the other members of the committee a good rule of thumb is to aim at a 10 per cent turnover each year. Renewal of the elected leadership is a responsibility of the leadership and should be consciously worked for. When likely talent is spotted it should be encouraged. Potential new officers and committee members should be asked to stand in advance of the AGM. The difficulty is of course that those already on the committee may be unwilling to stand down, and oddly enough it is usually those of least value to an organization who are slowest to recognize that room should be found for new talent. But in a committee which makes regular renewal a conscious policy and openly explores the possibilities at its meetings, it is less likely that an old guard will develop which considers it has a prescriptive right to a place.

Annual report
This goes to all the members whether or not they attend the AGM at which it is presented. It is another form of report-back to the membership at large and is therefore worth taking trouble over.

How long or elaborate the report is will depend on the size and ambitions of the organization, but there is no excuse for its ever being anything but cleanly typed and readable or adequately printed and laid out. The cost of doing the job properly is small and the benefit worth having. An added reason for a decent looking report is that it should also go to the press (see Chapter 3).

Like the AGM, the annual report has a number of formal jobs to do: it should list all officers and committee members; it should give the total membership of the organization; the text of resolutions adopted at the last AGM or subsequent general meetings should be given in full. The number of meetings held by the EC and other committees and the appointment of any new sub-committees (with their terms of reference) should be noted. A refinement is to list the attendances of individual members at committees.

In addition the report will carry an account of the year's work. A sensible method applicable to many organizations is for the Secretary to write a brief overall account covering the high-lights—the main victories and defeats. Sub-committee secretaries and specialist officers should contribute sections on their specialities. The Press Officer, for instance, may report the number of column inches of press coverage gained, the number and titles of press releases issued, and a comment on whether the reception of the organization's policies by the media has been generally favourable or otherwise.

The accounts and balance sheet should be included in the report, with a note on the financial position by the Treasurer. The report as a whole should be signed by the Chairman on behalf of the Executive Committee.

Sub-committees

Lucky the organization that never needs to appoint a sub-committee. All committees make work and paper, and the decision to appoint a new committee or sub-committee should never be taken unless it is absolutely necessary for efficiency. There are times when it is.

The golden rule is: give the sub-committee a specific job and make sure its terms of reference are clearly defined and minuted by the superior committee. Only large and permanent organizations need a panoply of permanent sub-committees. They are, for instance, useful in an environmental group which may want to have specialist committees on historic buildings, commons and open spaces, footpaths, new developments and so on. It would be sensible to appoint, for instance, an editorial sub-committee to prepare a pamphlet, or a research sub-committee to prepare material for inclusion in evidence to a public inquiry.

While the sub-committee is sitting it should report regularly to the main committee. The sub-committee's minutes should be circulated to the main committee and formally received. The chairman or secretary of the sub-committee should draw attention to any decisions requiring EC approval or others of special interest. When the sub-committee has sent its final report it should be thanked for its work and disbanded.

Membership

The variety of forms of membership available in voluntary organizations is sometimes bewildering. Here are the main types:

Individual membership, normally referred to simply as *membership*. Its sub-divisions are ordinary, married couple, youth or student, retired person, life membership. An ordinary member pays the basic rate subscription. If this is set at 50p per annum concessionary rates might be: married couples, 75p; students and under 21, 30p; retired persons, 25p; and life members a single payment of £12.50.

The most complicated alternative form of membership for individuals is what is usually called *associate membership*. Its purpose is usually to allow some members to be associated with the work of the organization without paying the full rate of subscription. For their lesser subscription they receive only part of the services or privileges of membership. For example a society charging a basic rate of £2 a year might supply its members with an annual report, a monthly newsletter and a free copy of any policy document issued by the society. An associate member, paying only £1 a year, might receive only the annual report and policy documents. A further complication is that some societies have associated members who are differentiated by not having full voting rights.

All this makes a lot of extra work: different membership lists have to be kept and the distribution of literature to members is complicated. Avoid it if you can.

But most local pressure groups will want to provide in their rules for other organizations to be associated with their work. Thus our hypothetical railway defence association will want to involve in its work the Women's Institutes, parish councils, local authorities and so on along the threatened line. And the choice here is between offering them *corporate* membership or *affiliated* membership.

A corporate member usually has the same rights as an individual member. The organization concerned will appoint one of its members to attend the appropriate meetings of the society of which it is a corporate member. Difficulties arise if corporate members feel that because they represent a large number of people they should have a special role in the organization, for example, an automatic seat on the EC.

For this reason it is often better to call this category affiliated members. Affiliation does not imply that the member is integrated into the organization as closely as if he is a corporate part, and consequently he will expect less. Often affiliation means no more than receipt of newsletters and an invitation to general meetings.

But if you have decided you want affiliated members presumably it is because you think they can be useful. In that case they must be provided with a place in the structure of the organization, where they can be made to feel at home while not being allowed to interfere too much. This is where a council concerning itself with general policy issues and receiving regular reports from the EC is invaluable. Affiliated members can be given an automatic seat on the council because, as this is not an executive body, it does not matter how big it becomes.

There is one other problem to settle about membership and that is the membership year. You can either accept individuals as members for twelve months from the date of joining or you can have a fixed membership year (coinciding presumably with your financial year) into which all members are fitted whenever they join.

If your memberships all fall due for renewal at the same time the Treasurer or Membership Secretary has to send out a lot of reminders and handle the inflowing subs in a peak. In a small organization this does not matter and is an easier system. The larger the organization's membership the stronger the case for having individual membership years, but this means that the responsible officer has to check his record weekly and send out the appropriate reminders to those who joined twelve months previously.

Name

A bad name will affect the group adversely as long as it exists. Get it right, and do not accept whatever somebody suggests at the public launching meeting. However good the suggestion may sound, leave it to the steering committee to settle, and let them have a careful think about it.

The name must satisfy two criteria: 1. It must sufficiently identify the organization and, if possible, its purpose. 2. It must come easily off the tongue, either in its full form or in an obvious abbreviation.

For example, the oldest and one of the most useful national environmental pressure groups is the Commons, Open Spaces and Footpaths Preservation Society. It owes its cumbersome title to the amalgamation of two organizations, one dealing with commons and open spaces and the other with footpaths. Abbreviation to initials produces the unpronounceable COSFPS, so the usual abbreviation is 'Commons Society' which implies a narrower range of concern than the society in fact has.

Regional amenity societies can content themselves with a single geographic title, for example, the River Thames Society or the Snowdonia National Park Society, leaving the preservation aspect to be taken as read. In the same field the Tyneham Action Group has a pronounceable acronym, as have the Defenders of West Dorset, though whether 'Dowd' gives quite the right impression is another matter. It is not worth while straining after an acronym if the short title or initials come easily off the tongue.

If you do get landed with an impossible title, and sometimes pedantic or internal political pressures cause this, get an official abbreviation into circulation as fast as you can. For my sins I once chaired an organization called The Save the Broad Street Line (Hampstead) Committee. The local newspaper properly bucked at this and called us the Save the Line Committee. which did perfectly well.

Reporting back

When the steering committee has settled all this it should call a general meeting of the organization to approve its proposals for the constitution and to tell people what it has been doing by way of action and policy since the launching meeting.

This second general meeting is a working meeting and will not normally raise the same level of excitement as the first one, but it must not be an anticlimax. If you had two hundred at the first meeting and there are only twelve this time the press and opposition are likely to draw unflattering conclusions.

This time you should have better organized publicity and more people will have heard about you. If you can get an attractive speaker to give a further pep talk, do so. Don't play the meeting up in the press beforehand; then, if a hundred turn up, honour will be more than satisfied.

To advertise the meeting you use the list of names and addresses collected at the first meeting plus any others you have collected since. There is no need for a house-to-house distribution of handbills: a few strategically sited notices will do in a tightly knit area. Press publicity will do the rest.

Until the meeting has approved the steering committee's proposals the organization can have no formal membership. So grab every member you can at the report-back meeting. See that the Membership Secretary or Treasurer is there with plenty of helpers and receipt forms to collect subs on the spot.

3
Publicity

Most pressure groups are presenting an unofficial point of view against the weight of officialdom. Government, central and local, has regular channels of communication with the news media, and usually has professional press and public relations officers at work to make the most of them. The local pressure group's great asset is that opposition is always news. Look at any newspaper and you will see that 'knocking' stories get more space and more sympathy than stories of people praising official efforts. By organizing itself to exploit this asset a pressure group can meet the biggest of battalions on equal terms.

But the group's publicity effort must go beyond sniping at the other side, however accurately. The group has a reasoned case to put forward. The publicity campaign must (1) demonstrate that there is widespread popular support for the case and (2) show that rejection of its case will be embarrassing.

The case can be put over in a variety of ways: through demonstrations, pamphleteering, evidence at public inquiries. In this chapter we study the most important way—publicity in the press and other communications media.

The Press Officer

This is the key job, and don't be misled by the title. He or she covers all news and comment media, television and wireless as well as the papers, and is responsible for advising the group on its relations with the media. But it is better to call him Press Officer than Public Relations Officer. To many newspapermen the latter term suggests the over-persuasive free spending of big business out for a free puff. Your job is to convince newspapermen that you have stories for them which are worth printing. Do that and you will get the space. Sympathy will follow.

Most groups conscious of the need for publicity make the Press Officer's job a separate appointment, but there is a case for combining it with one of the other offices. The Secretary will not have the time to do it justice, but the Chairman or Vice-chairman probably can, and the advantage is this: it enables the press to quote the group's spokesman as the Chairman or Vice-chairman instead of as its Press Officer. Newspapermen often prefer this because they feel that it gives the quotation more authenticity than if it comes from a nominated spokesman.

In any case the Press Officer must work from a position of strength within the group. If he is regarded as a mere manufacturer of news stories he will be largely wasted. The Press Officer must be involved in the central counsels of the organization. Obviously he has to know what is going on and be on the look-out for publicity material, but he should also be in a position to advise on the group's plans and policies as they are developed, so as to see that their publicity potential is maximized.

This does *not* mean that pressure groups should make policy decisions for the sake of publicity, but that often the way in which a policy is presented or the timing of an announcement or event can be improved so as to make it more newsworthy. For example: it would be foolish to hold a public meeting on a Thursday evening if the local weekly paper has gone to bed that morning (as many do). By the next week's edition the meeting will be stale news. The Press Officer should be alert to prevent an error of that kind, which could make the difference between getting three or four paragraphs of coverage and the front page splash.

Groups who have professional journalists, public relations men or ad men in their ranks will often appoint one to the job. But this chapter is a crash course on the Press Officer's job. *It is a job any intelligent person can do.*

Press releases
The key to successful press relations is the press release. Don't rely on telephone calls to friendly reporters, still less wait for

them to ring you up. When you have a story, put it down on paper and post or deliver it to them. What you send them is called a press release, or—in journalist's jargon—a hand-out.

The group should have special stationery for this purpose and it should be headed 'Press Release', with the name of the group alongside. The names and addresses (and telephone numbers, work and home) of an officer or officers of the group who can be contacted about the contents of the release should appear on it.

Even when you know your newspapermen well and they are telephoning your Press Officer every week to see if he has a story you should still use the release to convey your news. It has four great advantages:

1. It is a more considered statement than an off-the-cuff conversation. Writing the story down concentrates your mind and ensures that all the points the group thinks important are included. It is much easier for the Press Officer to check a script with other officers than to clear with them what he plans to say on the telephone.

2. Newspapers are notoriously inaccurate. The written word is more likely to be reproduced accurately than the spoken.

3. Because the release can (and should) be sent to all the media which may be interested in your news it saves time in making separate telephone calls or holding separate interviews.

4. By setting out the story from the originator's point of view the release makes it more likely that what the paper prints will bear the same emphasis.

The author of a press release should not aim to write what will appear in the paper. For one thing it will not be printed. No outsider can know how much space the page editor will have available. For another, any reporter worth his salt always re-writes a press release. So there is no need to attempt to write in journalese. If you are a journalist, well and good. If not, it does not matter. Put your story down in plain English and in logical sequence.

Plain English means just what it says, but logical sequence means the apparent opposite. Most of us, when telling a story in conversation or in a report or brief in our working lives, begin at the beginning and go on to the end. Newspapermen reverse this procedure. They put the news point, what to us is the conclusion of the story, in the first paragraph. Everything which follows is to a greater or lesser extent embroidery. There are two reasons for this. The first is that the introduction to the story is intended to grasp the reader's attention. The second is that a story once written by the reporter may change before it reaches the paper and again between editions. It has to be flexible. If important news arrives to crowd it out it may be cut to half its length or even to a couple of paragraphs. It should be so written that these cuts can be made very easily. Ideally, though rarely in practice, the sub-editor (see glossary of newspaper terms at Appendix D) should be able to chop the story at the end of any paragraph. The paragraphs remaining should still constitute a coherent story.

In Appendix C there is a model press release such as a local pressure group might issue. Read it carefully and see how far it meets these criteria.

A beginner's mistake is to worry overmuch about length. Newspaper stories are highly compressed and amateur authors of press releases sometimes think their copy should be the same. The rule is to keep it short, but say what you have to say. The newspaper will do the cutting and you never know your luck. Provided there is a genuine story there you will get coverage. In any case experience will teach you what is and what is not likely to make the paper.

Because you are amateurs and have to establish your newsworthiness with the recipients, make sure you get the form of the press release right. Use quarto paper. Type your copy and double-space it. Use one side of the paper only and leave a wide margin on the left. Keep to one or at most two sentences per paragraph. If you name anyone give their full name (first name if possible) and title. At the end of each page below the last line type the letters 'mf' (for 'more follows') and at the end type 'ends'. Sign your release.

All these instructions are designed to make your release easy for the newspaper to handle. Stories have to be cut up—sometimes physically—and new matter inserted. If there is typing on the back it has to be copied before this can be done. If foolscap paper is used cutting is less convenient. Instructions to the printer and interpolations have to be written in—hence the double spacing and wide margins. Copy may be sent to the typesetters in bits and pieces, so if there is more of a story to come they need to know. Paragraphs should be short because this also makes cutting easier, and anyhow newspaper paragraphs are short. First names are popular with newspapermen because they give a greater air of intimacy, and titles give the reader some idea why John Smith is pronouncing on a particular subject.

When you have drafted your release sit back and try to think of any questions not already answered in the release which a reporter might ask. Then put the answers in but make sure the press have your telephone number just the same.

Put a heading on your copy; not because this will be used in the paper (it won't) but to catch the eye and sum up the story.

Don't send the top copy of your release to one paper and carbons to others. Duplicate your typescript and treat them all equally.

Address your press release to the News Editor on a daily paper, the Editor on a less frequent publication. If it is especially concerned with picture material send it to the Picture Editor as well. Also send a copy to any reporter you know to be particularly interested in your news. But don't rely on sending the release only to him. He may be on holiday or assigned to something else.

A press release will do just as well for wireless and television; there is no need to write a separate piece.

Talking to the press
Using the press release as your normal means of communication will not preclude other contacts with journalists. But a good Press Officer does not thrust himself on newspapermen. If he is good at his job they will come to him.

The basic rules are: be available, be honest. Just by being available to talk to press men you are doing a useful job for your organization. They will want your comments on moves and announcements made by the other side. If you have time, put these in a release. If not, count on the press to ring you provided you have done your job properly so far.

Never exaggerate for the sake of getting coverage; in the long run you destroy your credibility. But remember that certain trigger words work wonders with the press: if something is 'new' by definition it is news. If you have had a working party taking the guts out of the opposition's case, call them a 'team'. If you can say this is the first time something has been done, do so. If your organization is making an appeal or demand, qualify it with the word 'urgent'. And so on.

The press
We will start at the bottom and work up. By definition the press that a local group will have most contact with is the local press, but you will want to know something about the nationals in case your campaign needs to attract publicity at that level.

Local newspapers
There are more than 1,400 local weekly and bi-weekly news-papers in Britain. They may be known half contemptuously and half affectionately as 'the local rag' by their readers, but they are vital to our sort of organization. The local weekly is read by everyone who matters. The Town Clerk, the county planning officer, the local MP will all read it thoroughly. For local councillors and politicians it is the only public platform to which they have continuous and easy access. They notice what is said in it and what it says. They are themselves anxious to figure in its columns as often and as favourably as possible.

Treat your local rag editor with respect. His goodwill can make or mar your campaign. Give him well-presented news in good time for his editions and he will give you fair and probably generous coverage, and this is half way to having his sympathy. If he is prepared to come out on your side in his leader column that is a big bonus. But let him get there in his own time. The man is entitled to make his own judgment—that's why he is an editor—and he won't like it if you give the impression of expecting his support as of right.

Remember that he works under great difficulties. His junior reporting staff are subject to rapid turnover, and often he will be relying on reporters who are still in training or barely out of it. They will make mistakes, like getting quotations wrong or misunderstanding a complicated argument. Correct these gently but firmly. Don't waste time squealing in the correspondence columns because you dislike the emphasis of a story or because it has missed out something you put in the press release. If you must write officially with a correction, go out of your way to offer praise as well. For example, 'In the generous and able reporting of last week's protest sit-in at Barchester Station there was one minor error. . . .'

The Press Officer's job is to get into the editorial columns of the paper. He should have a corps of volunteer members of his organization standing by to leap into the Letters to the Editor page as *individuals*, not writing on behalf of the organization.

The local rag is usually weekly, sometimes bi-weekly. Leisurely as this sounds compared with the schedules of a daily it still has edition times to meet. Feature pages may be set in type as much as a week before use. Other pages will have their own time-table; it is physically impossible for them all to go to the printer on the very last night before publication.

The Press Officer must know these schedules. If he thinks he will have a story at an awkward time but can do nothing to advance it, he should have a word on the telephone with the chief reporter or editor to warn him that something useful is coming.

Remember that a weekly covering a wide rural area will have editions special to certain districts. Two or three pages will probably be devoted to news from a particular district and these pages will be different for different parts of the paper's circulation territory.

It used to be said that every local paper editor had on his desk the slogan: 'Every name told is a copy sold'. Make sure that any copy you send in identifies local people. If you are mentioning for the first time Mrs Matilda Jones who raised £50 for the fighting fund, give her address and the number of children she has. If one of the kids helped her, mention which local school little Johnny attends.

Regional dailies

There are two sorts, evenings and mornings. The latter are especially important to any local group campaign outside the London area and the south-east.

Regional mornings are papers like the *Western Morning News* (Plymouth), the *Birmingham Post* and the *Journal* (Newcastle). They cover wide territories. The *Liverpool Daily Post*, for instance, circulates throughout North Wales. They have small circulations but they are highly influential. Their manner is usually extremely respectable and their politics conservative, but inch for column inch their standards of reporting are higher than any other section of the British press.

To these papers your stories will not be so important as they are to the local weekly, but they are very open to material which demonstrates that the paper is serving local communities. Well-written press releases are vital. Their timing is different from that of the weekly. For example: your public meeting is on a Tuesday evening; the local weekly will probably send a reporter anyway, if not, texts of the speeches delivered on Wednesday morning at the newspaper office will probably be in time (but get them in beforehand if anyhow possible).

The regional morning paper will quite possibly use the local rag reporter to cover the meeting for them, but they will want their story in the paper next morning, and 9.30 or 10 p.m. is getting a bit late for all except world and national front page news on this sort of paper. So it really is essential that your handout, giving as full texts as possible of the speeches, should be in the regional daily office by at least the morning prior to the meeting: earlier if you can. The advance copy does two jobs. It enables the news editor to decide whether the event is interesting enough to merit sending a reporter, and it means that some sort of story can be largely prepared in advance of the meeting.

The regional evening paper is a very different cup of tea. This is usually much more brightly written than the morning paper, which is often a stable-mate. Its circulation area is smaller, often only a single city and its immediate environs. It has less space for local campaign stories and is interested in lighter news anyway. But it will cover what the editor thinks is important to its readers. It will not of course simply repeat what the morning paper said the same day, but in many places the regional evening doubles for the regional morning, which has long since vanished.

The national press

If your campaign achieves national proportions you will need to treat the national newspapers as you would any other daily papers, but until that stage is reached, and while you are still trying to break out of the local level, the best tactic is to angle your material at particular papers or groups of papers.

Until you have achieved self-sustaining fame the popular press will only print stories about you that have a strong popular angle. If old Mrs Maggie Brown has been taking her basket of violets into Barchester on the train to sell in front of the town hall for the last half century, the effect on her of closing the line is an excellent *Daily Mirror, Sun, Daily Mail* or even *Daily Express* story.

The serious press will be interested in the passenger census figures, especially if these controvert rival statistics issued by British Rail. The environmental correspondents of *The Times* and the *Daily Telegraph* both devote a lot of space to local and regional environment stories and spend time gathering material from local groups.

The *Telegraph* favours stories with an anti-bureaucrat flavour. *The Guardian* is keen about civil liberties, equality of educational opportunity and so on. These are only a few of the more obvious traits displayed by different papers. An efficient Press Officer familiarizes himself with the styles and interests of papers other than the ones he sees regularly, and exploits them.

This is probably as close as we can get to answering the question many novice Press Officers ask: what is news? Or, how do I know when what my organization is doing is newsworthy? There is no all-embracing answer. In Fleet Street they define news as anything that interests the ordinary bloke who is not interested in anything very much. For your local paper it is the survey, report, census, speech, resolution, demonstration or row with the council your group has just made, held or provoked. The best working rule is to assume that anything your organization does is news. The Press Officer quickly learns what will get reported.

The local pressure group's problem is how to become national news. Most local groups, if their Press Officer is reasonably alert to the flower-seller type of story, can make the occasional mention in one or more of the nationals. But it may be that your campaign strategy requires you to be regularly and frequently featured in the national press. An example of this would be the attempt to reverse a ministerial decision taken after public inquiry—see Chapter 7, page 88.

No single heart-throb titbit is going to take you into national news status, though a series of them will be a big help. There are three ways in, any of which can work on its own, but are best applied in combination:

1. *The sheer size of your story.* The campaign against siting London's Third Airport at Cublington was a continuing national story simply because airports are big things and some millions of people were affected by the choice of site.

2. *The universal applicability of your position.* In itself yours may be a small affair, but if it clearly illustrates a general position which could occur elsewhere, e.g. through some loophole in the law previously unexploited or some novel effect such as a toxic waste in an apparently harmless industry, then Fleet Street may take it up.

3. *Scandal.* This does not mean catching the Minister in bed with the wife of the promoter of the disastrous redevelopment scheme your organization is opposing. But if you can show that Whitehall has ignored evidence you have brought forward, or that procedures designed to safeguard individual rights have been hurried or omitted, or that the official statistics are wrong, then you have a national story. And if, despite this, the official side persists with its plan, scheme, policy or whatever the story will get bigger.

All this is only common sense. Competition for space in the nationals is obviously more intense than in regional or local papers. There are scores of groups like yours up and down the country all trying to break through, and news editors can take their pick. You can help yourselves by playing initially on the known characteristics of different papers and by exploiting the papers' operational needs. The paper which reaches your breakfast table on Monday morning was written over the weekend when news is hard to come by. Parliament is not sitting. The week-long stream of press releases from Whitehall is stilled. There are no first nights, no stock market and few industrial stories. So Sunday is your chance. A release that would go straight on the spike (see Appendix D) any other day of the week may make the paper on Sunday night.

By contrast Saturday is the worst day for getting into the nationals. The number of pages printed is governed by the amount of advertising space paid for and this is always at its lowest on Saturdays when, the advertising agencies believe, the consumers are less likely to read their copy. So Saturday papers are editorially thin and competition for editorial space is fierce.

Do as you would be done by
You must treat the press fairly. It is one thing to send a carefully angled story about your local campaign to the *Daily Mirror* alone, but for your news stories you must treat all papers alike. Send out the same press release and make sure that it contains the whole story. It is up to the different newspapers to put their own gloss on it by ringing you up for additional material or by getting a line from the other side. If you are once caught out making favourites of one or two papers at the expense of others your credit will go to zero. It simply is not worth getting top of the page coverage from one paper in return for an exclusive if you thereby wreck your relations ever afterwards with its competitors.

Treat reporters right and they will return the compliment. You will find that you can develop a confidential relationship with reporters who trust you if you trust them. One aspect of such a relationship will be the freedom to talk to a reporter off the record. This means that you can tell him something which he cannot use in the paper but which may help him to understand an issue better or persuade him to take a more sympathetic view of your case than the publishable facts warrant. Use this facility with discretion and only if you have to. Off-the-record conversations are only acceptable to journalists if they recognize you as a valuable source of frequent hard news.

And the press can help you. A reporter who has received an advance text of a speech by a local councillor, who opposes your campaign, may give you a big enough hint of what it contains to enable you to have an instant reply when it appears.

In any case reporters who know you will start ringing up and asking for quick comments on the other side's moves and announcements.

These will have to be quick but don't rush into saying something silly. Make sure you have grasped what has been said or done. Then, if you need time to think or consult others, thank the reporter and promise to ring back in fifteen or twenty minutes. Keep the promise.

Television and wireless
So far as news is concerned these media have the same requirements as the press. Treat the local radio station, if there is one, as you would the local paper, but bear in mind that it will have its own schedules and deadlines related to the timing of newscasts. Treat the BBC and commercial television stations as you would a regional or national daily paper. Address material to news editors.

The big difference with television is that for optimum coverage your news must be visual. One public meeting looks much like another. It won't interest television producers very much. But demonstrations and marches are made for the medium, and the more unusual you can make them the better.

A local campaign's best chance of getting on to television is to plan a visual news story aimed at the box. A good recent example which also illustrates the influence which television can have on the local bureaucracy comes from the small town of Winslow in north Buckinghamshire. Here the local footpath protection group were campaigning in the summer of 1972 to persuade the county council to replace a bridge on a footpath linking two villages. Press publicity and complaints to the council had no effect. So the group staged a double march of villagers from the two settlements converging on the site of the bridge. BBC Television were invited and they filmed the scene for the regional evening magazine programme. Three weeks later a new bridge was in position.

Give television as much warning as possible of events like this. Television camera crews are expensive. The news editor must deploy them carefully and thriftily. The more notice he gets of likely events the better he can plan how to use his limited resources.

At Appendix E there is a sample press notice advertising a forthcoming picture story. This would be sent to both newspaper and television news editors.

When there is no visual story to be filmed television news editors and producers look for other ways to give the news visual appeal. Still pictures may be shown to illustrate the story while the newscaster speaks 'voice-over', or a news-maker may be interviewed, thus introducing another face and more variety to the programme.

It is vital for pressure group spokesmen using television to master the art of the interview, but it is not an art which can be taught. The most important single rule for beginners is to speak as colloquially and spontaneously as possible. Treat the interview as an ordinary conversation.

Remember that television screens come into living-rooms and kitchens. The interviewee who is bitter or angry or determined to say his piece at length and in detail, whatever the loss of clarity or degree of boredom involved, makes a poor impression. Though this is not true if anger or bitterness are seen to arise naturally in a news situation which provokes them. Television is the medium of the middle man. However extreme the statements you wish to make, express them as if engaged in a cosy domestic chat.

It is therefore worth taking some trouble to select the right man to serve as television (or radio) spokesman for the group when the occasion arises. He has to get it all into 90 seconds—three minutes if he is lucky. He must be concise, articulate *and* relaxed. A tall order. To fill it adequately be ready to ditch the man who thinks he should have the job, and pick your coolest, least anguished customer.

Miscellaneous publicity
There are plenty of ways other than the editorial columns of the press for taking your campaign to the public. Any local organization is likely to have to use some of them from time to time. Handbills to advertise a meeting and advertisements in the press for the same purpose were mentioned in Chapter 1.

But your main effort should be put into editorial publicity, because it is free and because it is, all in all, the most effective means available for presenting your case. The only alternative means by which you can keep your case in front of the public week after week is by paid-for advertising. This is obviously expensive and far less influential. Appearance in the editorial columns is taken—rightly or wrongly—as evidence of public concern. A full-page advertisement, however brilliantly laid out and cogently argued, is primarily evidence of your organization's wealth (one exception to this is discussed on page 56).

Two methods of advertising especially likely to lure voluntary organizations into pointless waste of resources are posters and car stickers. Somebody will almost certainly suggest one or both of these at the first committee meeting, if not sooner. It is almost certainly the wrong moment for either.

If your organization serves a small community which revolves around one obvious nucleus, then a score of posters in shop windows can be a quick and cheap way of announcing a meeting or demonstration. But this also illustrates the weakness of posters. They get their effect by repetition. They are not, as the newspaper is, something which people stop to read. They are taken in from the corner of the eye or subconsciously while waiting for the traffic lights to change. A persuasive poster to be effective must cover very densely the area you are concerned with. If it does not you are throwing your money away.

Car stickers are another popular idea which is only useful in carefully defined circumstances. Posters at least have the advantage of being on stationary sites. Car stickers spend a good deal of their time moving about and are very small. It follows that car stickers only work if they are used in saturation quantities. If every other car in town will carry your message they are worth while, especially during a fund-raising drive or when it is necessary to evince the maximum of solidarity. But 500 stickers spread round a county is a waste of good adhesive.

Newsletters
So far we have been looking only at external publicity, which is the most important kind. But the organization's own members must be kept informed of what is going on, and there is a limit to the number of general meetings you can hold and to the proportion of members who will attend them. Unless your group is a very small one, e.g. based on a few neighbouring

streets, it must have a newsletter or bulletin circulating regularly to the members.

As with annual reports the important thing is to make this clear and presentable rather than a marvel of fancy layout or jazzy typography. There are two basic alternative methods of reproduction:

Duplicated typescript   Most economic for runs up to around 1,500. The presentational advantage is that it looks urgent and newsy (more so than photographic reproduction). Capitalize on this by close typing and fill the pages completely. Use short punchy headlines to each item. A printed title on the top of the front page gives the production a lift.

Photographed typescript   For this you will have to go to a commercial printer or agency, while simple duplicating may be possible on a begged or borrowed machine. More scope for layout. Use Letraset or other proprietary brands of stick-down letters to create headlines. Type story underneath. The pages thus produced are then photographed.

A newsletter should be issued at least quarterly and it must have an editor who takes final responsibility for what goes in, subject to the policy guidance of the committee. Never have a committee to edit anything. It cannot.

Though meant primarily for internal communication the newsletter serves external purposes too. It should always be circulated to the press covering your campaign. Often a paper will use again material from the newsletter which it has already covered when the subject came out in a press release. The newsletter is also a handy give-away item for recruiting new members. It is probably the one tangible object which members receive in return for their subscription.

Manifesto
What other published material a pressure group produces will depend on the nature of the campaign. But one item is essential and this is a statement of aims. It is a give-away item to be used in making new members or for sending to anyone who inquires about the group. It may be a letterpress leaflet elaborately illustrated or a single side of duplicated typescript. In one form or another it is a must.

The very first meeting of the Executive Committee should settle the manifesto's broad contents and put production in hand. It should be ready by the time the Committee reports back to a second general meeting. It will be evidence of the Committee's activity and there will be plenty of people there ready to distribute the leaflet.

Bad publicity

All publicity is good publicity, say some people. This is rubbish. You want your organization's name and aims in the press as often as possible, but you want it there in an informative or sympathetic light.

Of course, unless your campaign commands absolutely universal support, in which case there is no need for publicity, you will be attacked. That is not bad publicity, because it mentions your case and you can reply. Bad publicity is publicity which questions the organization's motives or disputes the facts on which its case is founded.

If this sort of thing happens the only answer is to crack back hard and instantly. Never leave accusations of this sort lying around unanswered.

4
Money matters

The money local pressure groups need can be found in one of two ways. The ordinary running costs (hire of rooms, printing, stationery and such) can be met from subscription income (provided that subscription rates are fixed at an economic level) supplemented, if need be, by the occasional social event designed to raise £100 or so. But big special costs—project costs—must be met by special fund-raising efforts.

Many groups never need to think about the second type of finance at all, but every organization needs a minimum regular income plus an occasional booster.

The Treasurer and his job
The Treasurer of the group has the same relationship to its money as the Press Officer to publicity. He not only has to keep the books, he has to be deeply involved in all the group's plans so that he can warn it if they are overreaching themselves financially. But there is one big distinction between the Treasurer and the Press Officer. When an efficient Press Officer warns against a particular course of action the group should take very serious notice. When an equally efficient Treasurer does so, the group's reaction should be: 'Thank you for telling us. We shall go ahead as planned and raise the money we need.' Lack of money should never be a constraint, only a stimulus to raising it.

When choosing your Treasurer bear in mind what sort of financial needs your group may face. Anyone can keep books and sign cheques and I do not propose to offer advice on the simple techniques involved here. There is no shortage of individuals around in any group who are already familiar with them, and plenty of simple manuals on book-keeping for those who need to find out quickly. Your problem in filling this job will arise if you expect to have to go in for raising sizable sums of money.

In that case the Treasurer needs to be someone capable of talking money to the sort of people who have money. If yours is the sort of group that contains a stockbroker or merchant banker in its ranks then you will have no difficulty, but if you have members like that you are unlikely to have serious money problems anyway.

If your members don't run to this sort of expertise and the wealth that goes with it you must choose your Treasurer for his cheek as well as his probity, because the golden rule in raising money is never to be afraid to ask, and to be prepared to ask for a lot and not to be disheartened if you are rebuffed.

The routine of the Treasurer's job is straightforward. He keeps a record of the financial transactions of the organization. Where bills and receipts are involved he retains these for the auditors to examine annually. He sees that those officers and committee members who need it have a cash float and that these floats are properly accounted for. He sees that the bills are paid regularly and is responsible for drawing the necessary cheques on the organization's bank account.

It is a good rule, though seldom observed, to insist that all officers and other members of the group who spend on its behalf submit an expenses claim for every penny. In most voluntary organizations there are some individuals so devoted to the cause and so placed financially that they do not bother to claim all they spend on items like stamps and telephone calls and travelling to meetings. This may be good for the group's finances but it may also inhibit others who are less well off from offering their services.

The organization must have a bank account. Never let the Treasurer operate payments from his own personal account. The Treasurer should report the financial position briefly at each Executive Committee meeting so that members are always informed of the state of the organization's funds.

The Treasurer should never be allowed to sign cheques alone. This is for his protection as well as the organization's. At least two other officers should be nominated, either of whose signatures must accompany the Treasurer's, and specimens of their signatures will be supplied with his to the bank. The names of those who can sign cheques must be clearly minuted by the Executive Committee. Any changes in signatures must also minuted and notified to the bank. Confusion about money, even if the results are quite harmless, causes ill feeling very quickly. A few boring precautions are worth taking.

The accounts must be audited annually, and the only problem here is to decide at what stage you need a professional audit. Take the advice of the group's bank manager on this. As a rule of thumb I advise having a professional auditor from outside the membership of the organization as soon as annual income passes the £200 mark. Until then you can use any member of the society, such as a bank official, who is willing to do the job. But whoever does it must not be a member of any committee which has power to authorize expenditure, nor must he himself incur expenditure on behalf of the organization or receive payments from it in any business or professional capacity.

The subscription

The mistake is to fix this too low because the initial needs of the organization are small. Look ahead to what may be necessary rather than consider only the minor but immediate expenditures. For example, will your organization have to brief counsel at a public inquiry or engage consultants or go to the High Court? The subscription rate you fix is unlikely to cover the expenditures these procedures would involve, but if any of them are possibilities there will be research to be done and perhaps solicitors to be paid. A reasonable amount of cash in hand will be a great comfort, and enable you to proceed more boldly than if every first penny has to be begged.

There must therefore be very few pressure groups which can possibly manage on a subscription of less than 50p per head, and most will need more. A small tenants' association with only a watchdog role to perform might go as low as 25p. A regional amenity society should think around the £1 mark at least.

Remember not to fix the rate of subscription at the launching meeting. The steering committee should do this when they have had a chance to consider future prospects. Let them budget for their immediate needs and then add 50 per cent.

The Treasurer will need a supply of subscription forms. These can be duplicated, and might look like this:

EAST BARSET
PUBLIC TRANSPORT DEFENCE ASSOCIATION

I/We accept the aims and objects of the above Association and wish to become an individual member/corporate members.

Name of individual, organization,
authority or firm..
(block caps)
and therefore enclose cheque/postal order/cash for......p......

Date.. (Signature)......................................
(on behalf of, if not self)

The same form should be attached as a tear-off slip to the organization's basic recruiting leaflet (see page 45 above). The Treasurer will need receipt forms to be signed and sent to all members.

Becoming a charity

Pressure groups should consider carefully at the start whether they wish to apply for charitable status. The advantages of this are that charities are exempted from income tax and that members can covenant to pay subscriptions to the group for a minimum period of seven years. The income tax paid on covenanted subscriptions can be reclaimed from the Inland Revenue by the charity. This has the effect of making the individuals' subscription worth considerably more than if it is paid in the normal way.

At Appendix F we reproduce an article by the Treasurer of the Ramblers' Association (a registered charity) that appeared in the Association's journal during 1972. This was designed to explain to members the advantages of covenanting their subscriptions. It offers a brief guide to how the system works.

But note that the amount of tax reclaimable was that ruling in the summer of 1972 and may well be different when you read this.

The man who can confidently define what constitutes a charity does not exist. It certainly does not mean that your group must be devoted to relief of the poor or the disabled or the hungry, which are the commonest connotations of the word. The Charities Act 1960 defines a charity as 'a trust or undertaking, established for charitable purposes only, according to the law of England, and subject to the jurisdiction of the High Court'.

This definition immediately tells us that charities must be 'established'. Thus a committee without a constitution, consisting only of a few individuals chosen at a public meeting to conduct a brief *ad hoc* campaign, could not possibly qualify. But it does not tell us what 'charitable purposes' are. These are nowhere categorically defined, but the courts and the Charity Commissioners (the body which oversees the recognition and management of charities in Britain) have at various times accepted different purposes as charitable, and this is what we have to work on.

It is common to charities that they must be for the benefit of the community or for an identifiable section of the community. You cannot form a charity to serve the interests of particular individuals. Nor can a body become a charity if its purposes can only be achieved by changes in the law. The Charity Commissioners will not recognize as charities pressure groups whose work lies in lobbying MPs and Ministers to repeal or amend legislation or to get new legislation introduced. In practice a number of charities do find themselves involved in such activities, but only as a minor part of their total work programme. And the Charity Commissioners from time to time make warning noises about charities which they think have overstepped the mark.

Religious and educational objectives and the relief of poverty are recognized charitable purposes, and groups with aims in these fields should have no difficulty in securing recognition. But there are also a multitude of charities established for 'other purposes beneficial to the community not falling under any of the preceding heads'—to quote a governing legal decision.* It is into this category that the sort of pressure groups we are mainly concerned with are likely to fall. The Civic Trust model constitution for civic societies (reprinted at Appendix B) is so written as to ensure charitable status for those organizations adopting it.

If your group does not obviously fit into any of these categories how do you go about finding out whether you can be recognized as a charity? The simplest method is to draft a constitution in the light of the information given above, setting out precise aims and objects which you consider to be charitable, and submit this to the Charity Commission (14 Ryder Street, London SW1), asking for their opinion on whether a society adopting this constitution would be recognized as a charity. You will find the Commissioners most helpful in advising on the points where your proposals fall short or exceed what is necessary.

This means that the group committee should not seek formal approval of the constitution from a general meeting of members until they have got the draft constitution right from the charity point of view. If the constitution has to be amended to comply with the requirements of the Commissioners it will have to be taken back to yet another meeting for the amendments to be adopted.

To sum up: charitable status is financially valuable to pressure groups and worth taking some trouble to obtain. But bear in mind that it can inhibit certain forms of action.

Appeals
If and when the time comes to raise money over and above the income received from subscriptions, three things are essential:

1. To fix a target.

2. To know precisely whom you are approaching and to tailor your campaign to them.

3. To seek the money for a specified object.

The first category of potential givers consists obviously of the organization's own members. True, they already pay a

---

* Commissioners of Income Tax v. Pemsel 1891 (A.C.531).

subscription, and some will feel that they have thereby done their financial bit. But your members are also those mostly deeply committed to your cause, so they are well worth tapping again. Here is a possible letter to members appealing for extra help. Each one should be topped and tailed individually by the President of the organization or whoever else has the best pulling name.

EAST BARSET
PUBLIC TRANSPORT DEFENCE ASSOCIATION

(date)

Dear   ,

Fighting Fund

I am writing to you because the Association has decided to set up a Fighting Fund and I want your help as a member in building this up.

Of course you already pay a subscription to the Association and this adequately covers our normal costs. But as you will have seen in the Newsletter the Transport Users' Consultative Committee is to hold a public inquiry on whether or not the line's closure will cause hardship. On the Committee's recommendations hinges the fate of the service; so this is the crunch for our campaign.

The Association's Council and Executive Committee have decided that we must be represented at this hearing by counsel, and accordingly we have briefed Mr John Jones, QC, who is an advocate with a great deal of experience in these matters.

In addition the Association has commissioned Mr Peter Bowlby, Professor of Economics at Barchester University, to undertake a detailed study of the economic effects of closure on the district, and one of his assistants is preparing a cost/benefit study which will, we believe, demonstrate that the true social costs of closure greatly outweigh the direct financial savings obtainable therefrom.

In addition we are calling Mr William Hargreaves, FSA and former railway accountant, as a technical expert witness at the hearing to challenge British Rail's figures for the present costs of the line.

In other words we plan to mount a fully expert and professional case. We believe that the line is so vital to the people of East Barset that nothing less will serve. But presenting the case will cost money.

I should obviously be breaking professional confidences if I were to tell you the fees we shall have to pay these experts, but I can tell you that the total sum is expected to be not less than £5,000 and may be more.

Thanks to the past generosity of members and the tight control which the Executive Committee has exercised over expenditure since our foundation last year, we have some £400 cash available on call. Nor do we regard the other £4,600 as an impossible target.

The Association has nearly 1,000 members. If each gave £5 we should reach our target. But I realize that this sum will be beyond the resources of many, though others may be able to give more. Please give what you can. I shall personally acknowledge all gifts however small.

I am enclosing an envelope for your donation.

Yours sincerely,

etc.

This entirely imaginary appeal is given at length because it illustrates some of the triggers which make people give.

1. People like to be asked by somebody famous or well known and they like a personal approach. Snobbery is a powerful stimulus, especially to the well-heeled.

2. The potential givers are taken fully into the fund-raiser's confidence. The purpose for which the money is needed, how the sum asked for is arrived at and the present state of the Association's finances are all clearly stated. This especially appeals to the responsible middle-class folk who are the backbone of most appeal funds.

3. The sum named will seem big to most people. So it should.

Small targets produce small gifts. But the scheme is made to seem practicable and therefore worth helping by the breakdown into gifts per member needed to meet the target.

The appeal letter should be really beautifully produced. It need not be individually typed, but the type face chosen should be one of those which look like typing and the right-hand margin should be unadjusted. The salutation at the beginning of the letter and the sign-off at the end should be clearly in the great man's own hand and not facsimile. Special notepaper should be used with the other patrons of the fund named on it. For these you want again the most influential names you can command.

An average of £5 a head per member of the Association is too much to expect in such a cause, though it might well not be in a stockbroker-belt battle against an airport or motorway.

What other sources can be tapped? What interest groups as opposed to individuals will suffer if the line is closed? Will loss of the trains make it difficult for workers to reach a particular factory? If so, approach the firm and see what they are good for. This time the appeal should be made by a personal interview with the directors, and the man to conduct the interview should be a business man of similar standing. His appeal should be based on hard economic facts. For example: is it worth 1 per cent of their annual profits to keep the line going? Make sure you have looked up the annual accounts for the last few years before you decide on the percentage to name. And what about the business men in Barchester who may lose trade? The Market Stall Holders Association, the Chamber of Commerce? Tackle them on the same lines.

Fund-raising methods
The appeal by letters and personal approaches should be closely linked to fund-raising by other methods. The same style of publicity should be used. There should be only one fund total related to the same target.

Frequent announcements of how the fund is going should be made, using ladder diagrams. Fit the type of diagram to the object of the appeal if you can. In the hypothetical branch railway line example work out how much money you need per yard of railway (a £5,000 target for a 20-mile line works out between 14p and 15p per yard. 'How many yards of tracks will *you* pay to save?' might be the slogan).

The names of individual donors should be published from time to time. Nearly everyone likes to know that they are going to get their name in print. This is one of the very few occasions when it is worth taking paid advertising space in the local newspaper. Use it to mention everyone (unless they have specified anonymity) who has given so far. Do not mention precise sums given by individuals (though it is right to do this for firms and other organizations contributing), but lump together all those giving over £50, all those between £30 and £40 and so on, according to the kind of sums you are obtaining. The advertisement needs only a single title line in addition to the list of names and a bold challenge at the end: 'Have you given yet?'

Allied to this is the sponsored advertisement: a good way to give an initial boost to the appeal. The most notable exponents of this technique have been the Anti-Concorde Project, a national pressure group.

The sponsored advertisement consists of newspaper advertising space paid for by a number of sponsors whose names are listed on the advertisement. A brief message about the cause and the appeal appears at the top. Below, the copy says: 'The following have subscribed to the cost of this advertisement.'

To be effective you need at least a half-page advertisement, and though this costs money it is not beyond the reach of many pressure groups. For instance, a full-page advertisement in an evening paper (outside London and the main conurbations) may cost around £200. If 100 members will subscribe £2 each there is room in that space to name them all and include an effective appeal message or policy statement.

It is impossible to give a useful list of all the possible means of raising money. Most types of fund-raising event are familiar to most people. They range from coffee mornings to jumble and bring-and-buy sales; from sponsored walks to fairs and exhibitions. If your group is short of ideas they should read *Fund Raising for Small Charities and Organisations* by H. R. Humphries (David and Charles, £1.95). This is a sketchy book but it does mention all the well-tried methods and gives useful advice on the techniques. Also it is written mainly for those for whom fund-raising is a principal part of the organization's function, rather than a time-consuming chore to be undertaken as part of a larger campaign.

The important thing is to relate your fund-raising events to your cause. There is nothing more soul-destroying than just raising money. The job is immensely more attractive if it also creates publicity for the cause. If you have organized your housewife members to hold coffee mornings, lay on a slide show of pictures about your campaign and its objects for those attending. This immediately means that you can charge a higher price for the coffee. If you choose a sponsored walk * as a fund-raising method relate the route to your cause. In our hypothetical branch railway case the walkers would follow a route criss-crossing the line.

Fund-raising and the law
The law intervenes in a haphazard way to control or inspect fund-raising. The Acts of Parliament you may need to know about are: the Betting, Gaming and Lotteries Act 1963; the Police, Factories, etc. Miscellaneous Provisions Act 1916, which lays down regulations governing street collections; the House to House Collections Act 1939; and the Charities Act 1960.

But the great majority of fund-raising activities by small local groups take place without the knowledge or interference of the law and without contravening it. If you have a solicitor on your committee—and it's a useful move anyway—ask him to check the legal position about any project the committee has in mind. The main types of events where you will have to do with the law are:

Lotteries You can hold a small lottery, sweepstake or draw provided it is not for private gain and provided that the organization holding it is registered under Section 45 of the Betting, Gaming and Lotteries Act. Registration is applied for on a special form to the local authority, accompanied by a fee of £1.25. Registration is only granted to organizations conducted

* Do not attempt to organize a sponsored walk without first reading *Sponsored Walks Safety*, published by Walkaid, 67 Rupert Road, Sheffield, at 2p (but send stamped addressed envelope or postage costs). Orders for more than twenty-five copies are post-free.

'wholly or mainly' for either charitable purposes; sports, games or cultural activities or support thereof; other purposes not including private or commercial gain. A small lottery is one for which the gross receipts do not exceed £750, for which the top prize is not over £100, and for which tickets cost not more than 5p and all cost the same. Conditions for the conduct of the lottery are laid down, and a return must be made to the local authority within three months. On this return you will be required to state the amount grossed by the lottery and the amount appropriated for expenses and prizes.

You do not need to go through any of these procedures if the lottery or draw is a private one, i.e. confined to persons attending a particular function, being members of a club or society or employees of the same firm.

Unless you are sure your event is covered by the exceptions mentioned above check all the rules and regulations very carefully.

Street collections and flag days These must have the permission of the local authority and again a special form is provided. There are also quite strict rules about the conduct of such collections and sales. For instance, flag-sellers may not be stationed less than thirty yards apart and their collecting boxes must be securely sealed. Again, check the rules very carefully. Breaking them might not get you into serious trouble with the law but could produce nasty publicity.

House-to-house collections For this your organization must be licensed—the local authority and another special form. And once more there are a series of regulations to be observed, of which the most notable perhaps are that the collectors should have individual identifying certificates and a prescribed badge.

Possession of charitable status (see page 50 above) will ease the organization's path through all these complications, since the local authority will regard this as good initial evidence of bona fides. But in any case applications to and negotiations with local authorities take time. Planning flag days and collections will also involve the police, who are concerned about obstructions on pavements and traffic hold-ups. So the organizers need to allow plenty of time to get the project under way.

A general legal point to watch is that once your organization achieves an income from property or investments exceeding £15 a year it will have to be registered with the Charity Commission or, if it is an educational charity, with the Department of Education and Science. This is also compulsory if your organization holds a trust or has the permanent use of lands or premises. If your group is registered as a charity the further registration is not necessary.

Professional fund-raising
This is for the big boys only. Turn to the professionals if the sums you need are an annual income in tens of thousands, or lump sums of the order of £100,000 or more. Enthusiasts who use their wits and plan intelligently can usually manage on their own for the needs of most local pressure groups.

No professional fund-raising organization will lift a finger for you until it has carefully studied your structure and needs, a process which will certainly take a month or two and will cost you a sizable sum, even before a penny comes in. At the end of the survey they may say they can do nothing for you.

5
Demos

The campaign tools examined in this chapter are all intended to demonstrate the numerical strength and emotional intensity of public support for your cause. They are to be used at the point in the campaign when they are necessary. If your organization's immediate problem is to persuade the High Court to interpret an obscure sub-section in an Act of Parliament in one way rather than another there is no point in demonstrating, but if the judgment goes against you and as a result hundreds of people are likely to suffer inconvenience or financial loss then you should be campaigning to have the law amended, and the techniques in this chapter can be brought into play.

The methods described are mainly within the law provided that certain simple rules and regulations are observed, and provided that, if you are demonstrating in a public place or on the streets, you co-operate with the police in minimizing nuisance and traffic disruption. At the end of the chapter some methods are mentioned which could lay participants open to charges of trespass (a civil wrong, not a criminal offence) but which if responsibly conducted seem to me legitimate. What I do not describe or advocate are any methods which could constitute physical intimidation of opponents, or which might lead to clashes with the police or damage to property. Pressure groups owe whatever effectiveness they have to the structure of society which permits and encourages the free expression of opinion. To shift the argument from the level of persuasion to that of force is to undermine their own interest.

Mass meeting or rally
This is the easiest form of demonstration of numerical strength

to organize, because it is static and concentrated in one place. The basic requirements are a hall or site big enough and speakers attractive enough to draw and rouse a crowd. The criteria of success are the numbers attracted and the level of emotional unanimity achieved.

The drawback to the mass meeting in its simplest indoor form is the low publicity content for any except local news media. One mass meeting looks very much like another, and they are rarely occasions when anyone says anything new. The big risk—and it applies to most of the methods in this chapter—is that too few people will turn up. Advance publicity must therefore be extremely intensive, and the organizers should not go ahead unless they are quite sure they have a very attractive platform. Second-best speakers just will not do.

Advance publicity must employ all the techniques described for the launching meeting in Chapter 1. But this time the publicity must begin long in advance (at least a month) and continue up to the last minute. Every possible device must be used. Posters—judiciously where they will do most good; newspaper advertisements—so far as funds will allow; a loudspeaker van on the day; house-to-house distribution of handbills and so on. For this type of event everything depends on getting a large number of people together, and once committed to the mass meeting you cannot afford a very public flop.

The problem for all organizers of mass meetings (and this partly applies to other techniques in this chapter) is to give them point. A successful mass meeting is related intelligently to the campaign of which it forms part. Unless yours is the sort of campaign that can command national stars for its platform, potential participants will need to be convinced of the usefulness of attending. They will come to hear Sir John Betjeman on the rape of the Victorian High Street just because he is John Betjeman. But if your top speaker is the local backbencher MP you will need a clear tactical purpose for the meeting.

At Appendix G is the handbill which was distributed for an open-air rally and 'walk-in' held in the summer of 1970 to protest (in vain) against the plan to build a motorway across part of the Chiltern Hills. This illustrates very well the point just made. The rally was not held just for the sake of something to do or because the organizers of the campaign against the motorway had run out of ideas. It was held because a recent change of Minister opened the possibility of a change of mind and because the organizers knew that a powerful deputation from the Countryside Commission was shortly to go and see the new Minister to try to persuade him to drop the plan. The rally also filled the publicity gap in what was already an established national as well as local news story, which fell after the previous Minister's decision and the cries of outrage it provoked. Note that the reason for rallying at that point in time is explained in the handbill.

The speakers were all well known in the organizations holding the rally, and advertisement of the rally was confined to distribution of handbills to members of these organizations, plus some house-to-house work in the half-dozen villages immediately around the disputed motorway route. But the speakers were not national names whose appearance on posters would have drawn a crowd. The organizers rightly assumed that this would not matter provided potential participants were assured of the point of the affair. The 'walk-in'—through an exceptionally beautiful piece of countryside—was thrown in as an extra attraction and as a visual draw for picture editors and television.

Five hundred people attended the rally. It made the national press and Independent Television News and was extensively covered in the local daily and weekly press. The cost/effectiveness ratio of the rally was excellent. Expenses were very small: a matter of £50 for the 12,000 leaflets printed (though these could have been improved by the inclusion of a picture of the threatened downland), plus the charges for hiring the village hall (in case it rained) and public address equipment, which is essential in the open air. Organization involved the minimum of effort. Two or three officers of the Chiltern Society and Ramblers' Association dealt with the organization of speakers, writing and layout of the leaflet. Half a dozen were involved in house-to-house distribution of leaflets. A wider distribution was achieved by enclosing copies of the leaflet with newsletters or journals of the organizations concerned when these were sent to members in the normal course of events. A handful of individuals served as marshals on the walk and checked that gates were closed and litter cleared. Permission for use of the village common was needed from the parish council and the police were informed in case of traffic problems.

This example also illustrates other weaknesses and difficulties in the mass meeting technique. In the Chiltern case the participants were sent off on a six-mile walk when the speakers had finished, and no doubt many of them felt they were marching for a cause; in any case it was a lovely sunny day so they enjoyed themselves. But what happens at the end of an indoor evening meeting? At a launching meeting, or even an AGM, the audience can go away feeling that something has been achieved or at least some necessary business transacted. The best you can get out of a simple meeting is a powerfully worded resolution, a telegram to the Ministry or other authority. Only if your last speaker is a real spell-binder and uplifter can you avoid sending people out into the night with a sense of anticlimax.

An alternative to the mass meeting is the teach-in, which was a fashionable form of protest and participatory democracy a few years ago. For a local pressure group it has several advantages. Its purpose is—ostensibly—to inform. It does not therefore need to build up to a climax. It is spread out over a longer period of time than a meeting, for example, from 11 a.m. to 6 p.m. People come and go and it does not matter if the hall is barely filled at times and full at others. The teach-in can also perform a very useful function in enabling a variety of different aspects of a problem to be explored at leisure, and people on the floor to contribute more than is possible at a formalized meeting.

If there is a lesson to be drawn from this discussion of mass meetings it is that in general they need a gimmick or attraction additional to the meeting itself to make them really successful. If the gimmick directly relates the event to the cause so much the better.

Marches, parades, processions and motorcades
Normally the point of this sort of event is to demonstrate concern to possible onlookers and to provide a visual story for press and television. Banners, floats or placards are needed. These have to be prepared, and the organizers need to make sure that they all take the same line. If the route is along public

roads the organizers will have to negotiate with the police over the route and timing and they may, for very good reasons, not get quite what they want. Gathering and dispersal points are required, and careful control of participants.

Except in the case of trade unionists deliberately absenting themselves from work to take part, these events must take place at week-ends. The participants won't be available at any other time. But week-ends also pose visibility problems. A march through the High Street will attract little attention on a Sunday afternoon and may well be a practical impossibility on a Saturday. On the other hand Saturdays and Sundays are good days for catching space in the national press (see page 40 above).

There is no general legal requirement that the organizers of events in this category should seek police permission or approval for their plans, though in some areas there are local Acts of Parliament in force which require you to give notice of your plans in advance to the local authority. Since those taking part are passing along the highway, which they have a legal right to do, no breach of the law is necessarily involved, but if your procession is a large one it may well cause an obstruction of the highway by holding up traffic or pedestrians. An obstruction is an offence, and subject to a maximum fine of £50. Whether a temporary hold-up of the kind a procession is likely to cause is an obstruction or not is very much a matter of judgment. The police are not likely to take an adverse view if you have agreed the route with them beforehand and informed them of the numbers likely to be involved. It is always wise to do this.

If the demonstration is to listen to speeches at any point or to shout slogans outside the town hall for instance then the matter gets more complicated. A street corner or town square meeting, especially if some hundreds of people attend during a busy period of the day, is much more likely to cause an obstruction than the same number of people on the move. It is therefore wiser to choose a meeting place where you are off and away from the road and where you can be certain you have a right to be. But do not imagine that because the piece of land is common land, a town or village green, part of a park or even completely waste ground, that you can use it without permission. Someone somewhere will own it, and if it is public open space owned by the local authority there will be by-laws governing its use. These will almost certainly forbid *political* meetings.

Going on the streets will highlight the need for effective campaign symbols and slogans, if the group has not already devised these. One of the first tasks of the steering committee should have been to arrange for properly designed notepaper for the group. 'Properly designed' means that the artwork should be drawn by a professional designer even if you have to pay him to do it. The theme selected for notepaper should be used again in all published material. Think of any large organization you know and their symbol or house style of design and print comes to mind. Obvious examples are the symbol used by British Rail, the speedbird of BOAC or the two simple italic capitals of the Automobile Association. Every time you break into a new field requiring use of your house style, for example, a pamphlet, the display screens for an exhibition, the cover of a book or the heading of your press release stationery, go back to the original designer and have him devise it in conformity with the earlier material. This unity of design makes all your group's work more memorable and more instantly recognizable.

If this has been effectively done in the first place the problem of designing for a public parade will be half solved. There will already be an identifying campaign or association symbol available. If this is associated with a particular colour then the same colour theme should be used on placards and banners.

Slogans can be more varied. People like making up their own and anybody can chalk or paste big letters on cardboard. But there should be one or two main slogans, and these need to be well thought out. A kind of irresponsibility affects slogan writers. People who are normally entirely responsible suddenly blossom into libel and abuse when they start slogan writing. This may land your procession in trouble with the police or those attacked. A rule for all organizers of such events is to issue firm guidance in advance about the message to be put across, and to hold an inspection of all placards and banners before moving off.

About the slogans themselves the only possible advice is the

65

obvious. Keep them short, simple and strong. It is much better to say 'Save the Line', 'Stop the Motorway', 'Green Belt, not Profits', 'Education, Yes; Discrimination, No', or whatever, than to rack your brains to think up clever-clever punning phrases. Brevity is the soul of memorability.

Lobbying MPs

Local pressure groups are unlikely to want to hold meetings or processions near the Houses of Parliament. There are special rules about these if you do. But your group may very well wish to stage a lobby of MPs, generally called a mass lobby.

It is well known that any individual citizen may call at the House of Commons and send in a card stating his name and business and asking his MP to see him. A mass lobby consists of a number of people doing this simultaneously and with the foreknowledge of sympathetic MPs, who will have arranged for rooms to be available inside the House where the lobbyists can talk to members and vice versa.

Clearly mass lobbies are useful only to organizations which have a case that can be expected to attract the attention of more than one or two MPs and which require Government action to decide their cause one way or the other. To be effective the lobby's organizers must be able to muster a sufficient number of lobbyists—proportionate to their cause—to be impressive. This is unlikely to be less than several hundred, and for groups more than a short distance from central London this poses transport problems. The mass lobbies which get into the news-papers and on television do so by sheer weight of numbers, and their organizers either have a lot of members in the London area to bear the brunt of the day or they are wealthy enough to be able to transport coachloads of supporters from a distance, for instance, a major trade union.

The publicity value of mass lobbies, other than the very biggest, is limited. The national press is not likely to be attracted by a form of demonstration which has been used many times before, but the local and regional press will usually give such an event a good show, and if well organized the lobbyists can make an impact on MPs.

But lobbyists do not make an impression by going to the

House of Commons to shout abuse at Members who disagree with them. No MP need come and listen to the lobbyists unless he wishes to do so, and he is unlikely to be persuaded except by arguments cogently and reasonably put. This suggests that the persuasive value of a lobby is greatest when the organizers aim to move the minds of uncommitted members, rather than simply make a noise.

An example of the useful mass lobby held by a small local pressure group was that organized by the committees campaigning to prevent closure of the Broad Street–Richmond railway line in north London in 1964. The numbers attending were quite modest (only a few hundred) and no national publicity was expected or gained. But the lobby was the occasion of one previously uncommitted MP (incidentally a member of the then Government) declaring himself for retention of the line, and the event also served to give a sense of cohesion to campaigners from eight different boroughs who had previously operated in the main separately from one another.

No permission is required to hold a mass lobby, but neither can entry to the House be guaranteed if the crowds become too great. If crowds pile up outside the House the police will probably take action to disperse them. None of this need happen with a well-organized and good-tempered lobby. Sufficient rooms to accommodate the lobbyists should be organized within the House in advance, and the police should have been notified of the event and the expected attendance. The nature, size and timing of the lobby should be discussed with the Chief Superintendent, Cannon Row Police Station, London, SW1 (telephone 01-930 1113), or his representative.

If you want to get national publicity for a mass lobby you need to think of an angle to brighten up the old formula. This is not easy in the precincts of the House, where processions and placards are banned while the House is sitting. Nor can you hold a meeting, since all open-air processions and meetings are banned within one mile of Parliament north of the Thames if Parliament is sitting, if more than fifty people are involved and if the object of the exercise is to present any petition or complaint to Parliament. This means that you cannot march in column down Whitehall, though there is nothing to prevent those coming to the lobby from wearing placards announcing their purpose. They will have to leave them outside the House. It also means that the participants cannot assemble out of doors beforehand or afterwards, although there are plenty of halls available for public meetings in the immediate vicinity; for instance, Central Hall on the other side of Parliament Square and Caxton Hall a few hundred yards down Victoria Street.

The best gimmick for your lobby may lie in the nature of the participants. If the theme of your protest is 'Equal Rights for Red-Bearded Dwarfs' the sight of several hundred red-bearded dwarfs making their own way down Whitehall will be quite enough to make the national press and that night's television news. Groups representing the disabled have made effective and legitimate capital out of their handicaps, and so have campaigners for pre-school play groups, using the children on whose behalf the demand was made.

In 1968 the National Campaign for Nursery Education mounted an imaginative mass lobby in which part of Parliament Square was turned into a crèche for children accompanying their lobbying mothers. A few years later the same organization handed out forget-me-nots to passers-by in Parliament Square under the slogan 'Don't Forget the Under-Fives'.

Any reasonable opportunity to use children or animals in a public display should be taken. If this sounds cynical remember that all pressure groups, when they are seeking publicity, are entering the entertainment business. Newspapers are entertainment, television even more so. A touch of show business goes down very well with both.

But don't overdo it. Using children in a protest about schools or play groups is fine. They are obviously relevant. If a new motorway is going to destroy a country lane where the local children go blackberrying, that is fine too. But if you hang slogans round tots who obviously neither understand nor are affected by the issue you may get the wrong reaction from on-lookers.

Demonstrations
Generally a demonstration only means a mass meeting—usually in the open air—or march or procession. A slightly more specialized type is the demonstration which has a particular target representing or symbolizing the opponents of the

campaign. The classic examples are the Ban the Bomb demonstrations against nuclear or supposedly nuclear installations, and those directed at foreign embassies as symbols of their Governments' policies.

Although such action has almost always been associated with major national campaigns often carried on over a period of years, it is very hard to see what effect they have produced on the policies of the Governments against whom they were directed. One is left with the impression that the noisiest and most aggressive forms of demonstration characterize frustrated minorities whose members are concerned with self-expression rather than serious persuasion.

It is extremely easy for a local pressure group to fall into this error. Precisely because the group is small and local, and because its opponents are very much bigger battalions, members of the group may be tempted into a form of campaigning which consists of making angry noises rather than applying specific pressure at points where it will be effective.

Demonstrations which go beyond demonstrating and contain an element of violence or which seek to over-awe opponents risk being self-defeating. Let me give some examples (which are based on real campaigns) to illustrate productive and non-productive forms of demonstration.

A civic society is fighting to save from demolition an eighteenth-century house in a prominent position. The house has been left empty and the owner, who wishes to redevelop the site for its commercial value, hopes the council will say that the building is too costly to save and allow demolition to go ahead. It is unfortunately quite a common situation.*

An effective form of demonstration could well be for the members of the society to occupy the house for a few hours. This would be excellent publicity and would draw attention at national as well as local level to the threat. Of course the members would be committing a trespass against the owner of the house, but since they would do no damage to it it would scarcely be worth his while to sue them, and any legal action against them would be very poor publicity for him. This form of demonstration would harm nobody.

* Any group concerned with this sort of campaign should read *Preservation*, by Wayland Kennet, Temple Smith, 1972, £2.40.

Alternatively the same society might decide that it should demonstrate against the council, which it believed to be aiding and abetting the owner of the house. This demonstration might take the form of a prolonged sit-in or occupation of the council offices or the relevant part of them. At the extreme—imitating some recent student practice—cupboards might be rifled and papers examined in the hope of finding incriminating material.

Such a demonstration would be instantly counter-productive. It would stiffen the council's hostility and persuade many uncommitted people that the campaign was up to no good. It might also be positively harmful to many people. The efficiency of the local council, which has other things to do besides looking after historic buildings, would be damaged. The working lives of entirely innocent servants of the council would be disrupted.

Participation for ordinary citizens in the processes of policy making has had a considerable vogue in the last three or four years. This has been especially true at local government level, though the vogue has not yet produced very much in the way of concrete improvement for unofficial groups seeking to influence policy. Nevertheless the position of pressure groups which perform a continuing role within a particular field of interest has changed out of all recognition in the last fifteen years. This is most true of civic and amenity societies, for whom regular and constructive exchanges with local government councillors and officials, formal consultation on many issues and nominated places on council committees are now, if not commonplace, no longer exceptional.

But the problem remains for any new pressure group or any group launching a new campaign to break through a barrier of distrust on the part of local government. As well as showing that its own proposals are workable it has to demonstrate that it consists of reasonable folk who deserve to be listened to. The louder forms of demonstration have a place in this process, but need careful selection and management if they are not to be counter-productive.

6
The local authority

Local pressure groups usually deal most of the time with local government, and many such groups are born of public discontent with the policy or policies of a local authority. Town and county and district councils are the natural whipping boys of the angry protesters, who have a vast body of popular myth about the nature of local government on which to draw in making their protests. We all know—or think we know—that local authorities are staffed by the dimmest kind of bureaucrats and tea-drinking pen-pushers. We all know that the councillors are a byword, if not for outright corruption, at any rate for feathering their own nests through foreknowledge of planning decisions and development policy. Or, if you have the other sort of council, its members will be time-expired trade union officials who owe their position to the decision of a remote and obscure caucus in the local constituency party.

All of this may be true of some councils and some councillors. As a characterization of all or most councils it is wildly false. And, as Wayland Kennet forcefully points out in his excellent handbook *Preservation*, when it *is* true it is your fault and mine. Whatever their shortcomings local councillors are people who have decided to sacrifice a lot of time and hard work to the community at large. This should at least temper our feelings about them. But the fact of their election and self-sacrifice gives councillors no divine right to be infallible. It certainly gives them no right to disregard the reasoned criticism of a pressure group.

The most satisfactory feature of local government from the pressure group's angle is precisely that it is local. Ministers can refuse to see deputations and give off-putting replies to questions in Parliament, but it is very difficult for local councillors and their officials to avoid direct contact with local people who wish to press them.

It is not necessarily fear of losing votes at the next election which makes local councillors more receptive to pressure. Local elections tend to be even more politically predictable than parliamentary ones. The pressure group which has to deal with a politically volatile council is fortunate, and should exploit the election fear of councillors to the full. What makes councillors amenable to pressure is that they have to live in the community they serve. A planning or housing committee chairman who refuses to listen to those objecting to his policies will be quickly branded as pig-headed by the local press, and he or she is not going to like that.

But it is also the nearness of local government which produces its most unsatisfactory feature, and this is the direct personal interest which members of local authorities have in the effects of their own decisions. At its worst this is exemplified by the speculative builder who serves on the planning committee. He may religiously absent himself from the discussion of planning decisions in which he is himself the applicant, or where his firm will do the building if the application goes through; but the old boy network being a fact of life he will nevertheless gain advantages from his membership of the committee, not least that he will have a say in general planning policies, and can try to steer them to the benefit of himself and his colleagues.

Less obviously councillors may vote to route traffic through one part of the borough rather than another because they do not want it near their own homes or, for similar reasons, a bias may emerge in the provision of schools or welfare facilities. Watching for and exposing bias of this kind is something any pressure group needs to be alert to.

How local government works

In Parliament executive power belongs to Ministers who report to the whole House. In local government executive power resides in committees, each dealing with a particular subject or related group of subjects. The nearest equivalent to a Minister is the committee chairman, who will usually wield considerable influence and who, in consultation with officials, will often take executive decisions between meetings of the committee. But committee chairmen are different from Ministers in the key sense that they are not members of a Cabinet taking collective responsibility for decisions. Nothing quite equivalent to Cabinet power at local level exists. The finance committee may come close to it in some authorities—but not if the council is divided on party lines, since some members of the committee will habitually dissociate themselves from the majority decision. In so far as collective responsibility for the authority's actions lies anywhere it lies in the caucus of the ruling party (if there is one).

The relationship between the committees and council officials is broadly similar to that of Ministers and civil servants. The committees make policy, the officials carry it out; but, as in Whitehall, officials often have a very big hand in policy making.

Committee structure varies greatly from one council to another. There are certain committees which every local authority must have by law. For example, every local education authority must have an education committee and every county and county borough must have committees especially charged to look after the authority's health and welfare services. County councils must have finance committees.

The first classification of committees is therefore between those which are statutory and non-statutory. But this classification does not affect the powers exercised by a committee. These depend on its terms of reference and what decision-making powers are delegated to it by the full council. Broadly speaking a council may delegate to a committee any powers except those of raising money by rate or of borrowing money. Beyond that what is delegated is a matter for the council to decide. The size of the council's work and the geography of its territory are the main determining factors. The greater the volume and complexity of the authority's work the more it is likely to delegate to committees. The greater the geographical spread of the council's territory, and the more difficult it is for members to attend meetings at a central point at, for instance, the county town, the more decisions will be finally taken in committee.

The second classification of committees is a functional one between vertical committees, which deal with a particular department or departments of the authority's work, and horizontal committees, which are concerned with one aspect that affects all departments. A finance committee is horizontal in that its work impinges on all parts of the council; an education committee is vertical.

In a council whose membership is wholly or mainly divided on party lines membership of committees will be settled by the party caucuses, that is, meetings of the councillors of each party. Members will be nominated broadly according to the strength of party representation on the council as a whole, and it is now usual for committee chairmanships to be held only by the ruling party.

In non-party councils membership and chairmanship may seem more haphazard, but will usually reflect broad areas of interest. Whether a council is party-controlled or not the more important committees usually achieve a fair distribution of members according to the wards or electoral divisions they represent.

Co-option to committees

Councils have power to co-opt members to their committees other than elected councillors (or aldermen). In some areas of local authority work this practice is long established. It happens quite frequently on education committees, and a quirk of the law requires it to happen on allotment committees.

It is beginning to happen on planning and countryside committees. But what is still rare on these is the co-opted member with the right to vote. Indeed most countryside committees are shadowy bodies, which are really only sub-committees of the planning committee plus some naturalists and amenity society people. A non-elected member may have full voting rights on such a body but this is of little use unless the superior planning committee delegates real power to it.

Co-opting a member of a local civic society or branch of the county preservation society to planning committees is relatively common, and is something many pressure groups would welcome. But it does have dangers. If, for instance, the civic society is invited to nominate a member of the borough planning committee he or she immediately becomes privy to a lot of information and advice prepared for the committee which is issued to members of the committee in confidence. How far can a person who is supposed to respect these confidences do his job for the nominating society? Unless a very tough-minded representative is appointed the society ends up by being dissatisfied because the member acts as a council spokesman, or the council feels that the society do not really wish to co-operate constructively in decision making.

How representative?
Far too many local authority committees and full councils meet at times which make it impossible for many members of the public or would-be councillors to attend. Afternoon meetings ensure that the council will be dominated by those who feel able to come at that time of day: the self-employed, women without small children and those so senior or so junior in their employment that they can get frequent leave.

Local authorities are in any case very unrepresentative of the social structure of the people they represent. The Redcliffe-Maud Royal Commission on Local Government found that only 12 per cent of councillors are women, that the average age is fifty-five, that only 5 per cent of male councillors are under thirty-five and one fifth are retired. It may be that a similar analysis of MPs would reveal equally startling imbalances, but one of the defences made on behalf of local government against its critics is precisely that it is more representative than Parliament and that councillors really do speak for those who elect them. The social composition of councils and the very high rate of abstention in council elections show these statements to be very dubious.

It is in any case quite impossible to talk about local councils as such, as though their representative or unrepresentative nature was more or less the same whatever the authority. There are great variations in the number of people a councillor represents. The Royal Commission noted that in Lancashire County Council there is one councillor for every 14,000 people. In Radnorshire there is one for every 430. These are the extremes, of course, but obviously the measure of influence that individuals and groups can exercise over a Radnorshire councillor is potentially very much more direct than anything that can be achieved in Lancashire. Note the word *potentially*. In practice these particular disparities may not make so great a difference as the mathematics suggest.

All these are points which local pressure groups should examine. Remember that your council is unlikely to have made the decision that annoys you without thinking. They will have a case for it—perhaps quite a good case.

If you can show that the council is unrepresentative because it meets at a time when the public cannot attend or which excludes potential members, do so. Analyse the membership. If you are campaigning for comprehensive schools and most of the education committee send their children to the grammar, or if you are complaining about the state of country footpaths and a third of the council are farmers or landowners, make these facts known. To demonstrate the bias of the decision-makers is half way to getting the decision changed.

The motto for handling councillors therefore is to treat them with just as much respect as they earn and not a scrap more. But don't needlessly put them against you. There are certain emotive causes which can be used to attract councillors' support even if, other things being equal, they might otherwise be against you. Councillors do often see themselves as village Hampdens standing four-square for local rights against the big battalions. If your cause can be represented as that of the small and weak against the great and powerful the chances of your local authority actively supporting it are at once immensely increased.

Council officers
It is all very well for a small local pressure group to speak contemptuously of bureaucrats in Whitehall; bureaucrats in Whitehall are used to it. It won't help to put them on your side, but they have armour thickened by years of abuse and your pinpricks will scarcely penetrate.

Local government officials are in a different case. If you refer to the new road plan produced by the council as 'an abortion which has clearly been prepared by incompetent engineers' you are not blackguarding a vast hierarchy of engineers in the Department of the Environment, you are probably criticizing a plan which the county or borough surveyor has drawn up personally.

Not only does this make an enemy of the surveyor but it is also likely to rally his committee to his support. The relationship of council committee members with their chief officers is close. The county surveyor attends every meeting of the highways committee, sits beside the chairman and advises him quietly, and speaks to the committee about new schemes. He is likely to be on first name terms with half the committee. Abuse will only have the very natural effect of making the committee feel protective about him.

Local elections
Local elections are important opportunities for pressure groups and should always be exploited to the full.

Questionnaires These should be issued to all candidates well in advance of the election. They should probe candidates' views on issues of concern to the group.

The results should be released to the local press and distributed to members a week before polling day. Candidates should be informed on the questionnaires that their views will be given this publicity.

Preparing a questionnaire is straightforward. You know what you want to ask about; just put the questions down in plain English. Avoid loaded questions: for instance, 'Do you support the Ministry's proposals for X or the alternative plan put forward by the Y society?' is right; wrong is, 'Do you agree with the Y society that the Ministry's proposals for X will be disastrous to the life and prosperity of Blanktown?'. This is an occasion for finding out attitudes. Reserve the propaganda for what you do with the answers.

Be careful how you handle the questionnaire's results, especially if most candidates for your council are party nominees. In fact the number of members of your organization who habitually vote for one party, who will switch their vote because of the answers given in your questionnaire, is minute and almost certainly not enough—unless the electoral division is highly marginal—to alter the result. If, in presenting the results of the questionnaire, you say too bluntly that the Tories support your cause while Labour does not (or vice versa), you will alienate potential supporters who put party allegiance first, and achieve no other useful result.

A better way to handle the result is to classify the candidates according to whether their answers were Very Good, Good, Satisfactory, Bad, or Very Bad, from the organization's point of view. Assign each candidate to one category or the other on the basis of his answers, but do not attempt to distinguish by party labels. Leave the readers to work out for themselves whether one party is more on your side than the other. Above all make sure that your classification can be minutely justified from each candidate's answers, and be prepared to make the detailed answer of any candidate available to anyone who wishes to see it.

Public meetings   The traditional time for questioning candidates about their attitudes to local issues is at pre-election public meetings. Today you may well find that your candidates hold no meetings at all, knowing that they are likely to be ill attended and that more useful contacts with the electorate can be made by canvassing. If a candidate is holding a public meeting by all means use it, especially if he is one whom your organization is anxious to force to declare his views or whom you wish to challenge publicly. But if you undertake this exercise, do it properly. It is no use sending one or two people along to such a meeting. They will be able to ask only one or two questions, and a skilful debater, under the protection of a sympathetic chairman, will easily evade the issue. You need perhaps a dozen in the audience so that the candidate is never let off the hook, and you will be wise to let the press know of the exercise in advance. This is a method to be used only where a candidate's attitude is positively shifty. If it is used against a reasonable candidate—even though he disagrees with you—the result may well be to create sympathy for him.

Elections   The fact that few voters will switch party allegiance on the particularist issue of any non-party pressure group is no reason why the group should not itself consider running candidates. Candidates do not have to come within a mile of winning to be an awful nuisance to candidates with a real hope of being elected. In a party-controlled council select marginal wards for your candidates, and choose people who will most obviously take votes away from the candidate you wish to shake up. You may well secure concessions before close of nominations. There is no deposit to lose in a council election.

There is no special mystique about an election campaign. Any well-organized pressure group can run one, probably at least as efficiently as the local political parties, especially if it concentrates its fire on one or two seats.

You need:

An agent   The agent is the man who takes the legal responsibilities * and masterminds the campaign. During at least the three weeks before polling day he should—if anyhow possible —be full-time. But plenty of elections have been won with a part-timer.

Headquarters   At least one room available throughout the day every day during the campaign, as centrally placed in each of the divisions you are fighting as may be. The bigger the territory your campaign covers the more necessary it will be to have sub-committee rooms.

An election address   This is your candidate's basic propaganda document setting out his platform, and should be sent to everyone on the electoral roll in the division. (There are postal concessions for electoral purposes.)

Voting cards   These go out to all electors listed on the electoral roll (or register), and are printed in your campaign colour. They bear the electoral number of the voter to whom it is addressed, and the number is obtained from the electoral roll. The purpose of this appears later.

Volunteer canvassers   Their job is to take a section of the electoral roll and visit each household and ask for support. For established political groups the aim of canvassing is to record who is for you and who is against, but a pressure group with no established voting record will find its canvassers using the canvass to persuade rather than simply record. Mark supporters F, opponents A and uncertains D (for doubtful). Sections of the electoral roll should be pasted on cardboard for convenience.

* The agent will find *Conduct of Local Elections*, published by the Labour Party, Transport House, Smith Square, London SW1, a useful guide. For parliamentary elections *Conduct of Parliamentary Elections*, 50p, from the same source, is equally useful.

The names of supporters should be marked on master sheets of the electoral roll at HQ. From these master sheets lists of supporters by streets or groups of streets are prepared. These should be written in a looseleaf note pad of the kind with a number of carbon sheets between the pages so that four or five copies of each list are made simultaneously.

Tellers These are the volunteers who sit outside the polling station (you will need a rota). The teller records the electoral numbers of voters as they leave. Most voters do not mind giving this information to the tellers. Some will try to give it exclusively to the teller from their party or organization working for their candidate, but the tellers always pass on the information to each other. As often as possible a runner takes the lists of electors thus obtained back to HQ.

Knocking up As the numbers come in from the polling stations the HQ volunteers cross them off the master sheet and the lists on the carbon pads. In the early evening the volunteer knockers-up come on duty. Each is given a sheet or sheets off the carbon pads. Typically this will contain perhaps twenty-five names scattered through half a dozen neighbouring streets. Perhaps six of these will have been crossed off. The rest have not yet had their electoral numbers recorded at the polling station exit and so have presumably not voted. The knocker-up's job is to remind them to do so.

When the knocker-up returns to HQ having contacted as many of his list as possible he can be given a fresh sheet, either the carbon of the one he has just done—but with more names now crossed off—or that for a different area.

This is a very brief outline of election practice. It is based on the assumption that sufficient volunteers will be available to fulfil the three functions of an election organization: to persuade, to record and to remind. A local pressure group may well not have available the manpower resources implied in this outline, though these requirements may not be as formidable as they sound. For example, a parish council election in a village of 500 voters could be run with a polling day staff of a dozen very comfortably. On the other hand the ward of an average London borough would require perhaps forty people for effective campaigning on polling day.

Lack of manpower on this scale should not of itself prevent an election being fought if your organization thinks it can field enough workers to make an impact. The purpose of electoral intervention may be to shake up local politicians as much as to win.

Reorganization of local government
Most of what is said in this chapter will remain valid after April 1974, when the reorganization of local government comes into effect. Boundaries will be changed and the powers exercised by different levels of local authorities will be shuffled, but the committee system and the relationship between councillors and officials will remain essentially as they are now. Local pressure groups will find that the following changes affect them particularly:

Size of authorities The principal effect of reorganization is to merge the big urban county boroughs (which have been unitary authorities responsible for all services) with the former counties. The counties were upper-tier authorities with lower-tier district councils carrying on functions beneath them. It is the latter pattern which will be followed now. The new counties will be upper-tier authorities. The new districts within them will be much bigger and more powerful than the old urban and rural districts, but no authority will possess the all-embracing power of the old county boroughs. There will be special metropolitan county councils (somewhat similar to the Greater London Council) for the main conurbations: Merseyside, South Yorks, Greater Manchester, Tyne and Wear, West Midlands, West Yorks.

Politics The old rural counties and district authorities were the strongholds of the view that party politics should be kept out of local government. The old county boroughs were fought almost entirely on party lines. The effect of merging the two will almost certainly be to introduce party politics to hitherto 'pure' areas.

Social mix Countryside environmental groups will find that the social mix of councillors on the new county authorities is very different from that of the purely rural past. The injection of major urban areas into the county structure will ensure this.

Publicity   An important provision of the Local Government Act 1972 is that the right of press and public to attend all council meetings is extended to all council committee meetings, unless the committee concerned specifically resolves that they should be excluded. This means that council committees can no longer have standing resolutions to exclude press and public from all or part of their proceedings. Such exclusion will now require a separate resolution at each meeting.

Councillors and aldermen   The councillors' term of office is extended from three to four years, and aldermen are abolished (except in London). Authorities will be able to confer the title 'honorary alderman' in recognition of services to local government.

Where power will lie   The overall effect of reorganization will be to place broad planning powers in most fields in the hands of the counties and day-to-day executive powers with districts. But this is only a very rough approximation to what will happen. The new division of powers is the result of prolonged horse-trading, pressure and counter-pressure between central government and the local authority associations. The main division of powers is set out in Appendix H.

7
Public inquiries

The overwhelming mass of public inquiries are sponsored by the Department of the Environment, and deal with appeals against planning decisions by local authorities. These are usually brief one- or two-day affairs. The other major category of DOE inquiries is that concerned with the Department's own plans, e.g. a new motorway or an airport site.

There is, however, a host of subjects outside the planning field on which inquiries can be held. Local authority by-laws are subject to confirmation by the Home Office, and the Home Secretary may hold an inquiry if he thinks the objections need this form of investigation. In 1967, for example, the Home Secretary held an inquiry into Rugby Borough Council's proposed by-law which would have abolished a central taxi rank under the Town Police Clauses Act of 1847. In the end the by-law was not confirmed. In 1972 the Home Secretary refused after public inquiry to confirm by-laws proposed by Brecon County Council for the control of powered boats on Llangorse Lake in the Brecon Beacons National Park.

Amalgamation of police districts, individual grievances about the workings of social security benefits, accidents of various kinds, public path extinguishment and diversion orders, the scheduling of ancient monuments, the siting of approved schools and prisons—all these are from time to time topics for public inquiry.

There are two myths about inquiries. Some people say they are a waste of time and some people see them as the means of reversing official planning or thinking.

It is true that in the commonest form of inquiry the original policy is confirmed in the overwhelming majority of cases.

These are inquiries into appeals against planning decisions by local planning authorities, and the allied case in which there is no appeal but in which the Secretary of State for the Environment 'calls in' a planning decision to determine it himself and, before doing so, holds an inquiry. About 25 per cent of these appeals are successful. In the remainder the Secretary of State or (with developments affecting ten houses or less) his inspector upholds the planning authority's decision.

This type of appeal inquiry is not likely to involve a pressure group. Only the applicant for planning permission has right of appeal against the authority's decision. If the authority grants a permission of which the local civic society, for instance, disapproves the society has no redress. It cannot appeal. The society's proper course is to be alert to the possibility of the permission being granted and to make such a fuss about it before the planning authority makes a decision that either the authority refuses the application or the Secretary of State calls it in for personal decision.

The fact that the great majority of planning appeal inquiries result in no change proves nothing about the efficacy of the inquiry procedure. These are—overwhelmingly—small cases affecting perhaps only a single building or an acre or two of ground. There would obviously be something very badly amiss if Ministers regularly held that the local authorities were making the wrong decisions.

The myth that inquiries are a waste of time begins to be persuasive only when we look at the bigger issues, the inquiries that run for a week or a month or more and make national headlines. Consider, for example, a very common form of inquiry procedure: that which takes place under Section 279 of the Highways Act 1959 into the routing of new roads. In these cases the Department of the Environment must hold an inquiry if there are objections to the proposed new road from a local authority. It has discretion whether to hold an inquiry if the objections come only from individuals, voluntary societies and parish councils.

The waste of time argument arises because in these inquiries the route proposals under examination are those prepared by the Department of the Environment or its agents, the road construction unit or county council, and the decision will finally be taken by the Secretary of State for the Environment. So—the argument goes—is not the Secretary of State judge and jury in his own cause?

This argument fundamentally misunderstands what public inquiries are for. A public inquiry is not a court of law with the Minister judge hidden away in Whitehall waiting to pronounce his verdict at a later stage. The object of most inquiries (and all those in the planning and related fields) is to inform the Minister of the nature of the objections and support a particular proposal evokes. Of course it is the Secretary of State who organizes a public inquiry into a motorway scheme, because it is the Secretary of State who has to make the final decision and must be informed of views for and against and possible alternative routes which people may wish to put forward.

Those who feel that they get a raw deal out of public inquiries usually expect too much of the process. It is, after all, very unlikely that the Department of the Environment, having spent years planning a motorway route and doubtless having a pretty good notion of the objections to it, will be persuaded to change its mind radically by an inquiry. What persuades Minister and Ministries to change their minds is political pressure.

But the ordered and more peaceful argument of a public inquiry has its uses. If you are opposed to the new motorway being built at all you are most unlikely to persuade the inspector to agree with you. Neutral he may be (and in a road inquiry he is not a member of the Department of the Environment inspectorate as he would be in a planning appeal) and open-minded, but he will work within the framework of Government policy, which is to build more motorways. At the inquiry into the designation of the Milton Keynes new city in 1967 the inspector expressed his own personal reservations about the building of new towns on such a large scale, but he accepted that it was Government policy to do so, and added: 'I should not consider it proper for me to report against the principle of the proposal unless there were some quite overriding argument against applying the principle to this particular site.'

Some of the objectors to Milton Keynes (notably a local pressure group called the North Bucks Association) were opposed to the new city being built at all. Obviously an inquiry conducted on this basis had nothing to offer them. But there were others, the National Farmers' Union, for example, and the small Calverton Residents' Association, who were prepared to take the inquiry on its own terms and argue for modifications in the Government proposals, and these they succeeded in some measure in obtaining.

This illustrates very well the kind of success which pressure groups may hope to obtain from a public inquiry. Going back to the motorway example: it is usually pointless to go to an inquiry to argue either that the motorway is unnecessary (because the Government have already decided it is and have committed expenditure to it in the roads programme), or that the whole road should be shifted six miles to the north (because the Department will have considered a whole corridor width of possible routes and firmly rejected the main alternatives). But it does make very good sense to use the inquiry to press for a re-routing of part of the motorway, perhaps diverging up to a mile or half a mile from the Department's plan at one point. Concessions of this sort are made. A motorway scheme may be altered, as the M 40 at Beaconsfield (Beaconsfield and Gerrards Cross by-pass) was, to minimize farm severance and the impact of the scheme on particular dwellings.*

This commentary on the value and limitations of public inquiries would be very complacent and unhelpful if we accepted that the public inquiry and the ministerial decision which flows from it must necessarily be the hinge of a pressure group's campaign. Of course where a pressure group is seeking only a minor modification of the whole scheme (for instance the Calverton Residents' Association's case for exclusion from Milton Keynes), the public inquiry and the presentation of their case to it are the climax of their campaign. But for the Stansted and Cublington campaigners against London's Third Airport the inquiries were only a single phase in a prolonged campaign, the efficient ingredients of which were not the calm rehearsal

* Since this passage was written the prospects of curtailment of the motorway programme have grown and the abandonment of some schemes can be expected. If this happens it will not be the result— as some protesters may imagine—of pressure at local inquiries, but of national factors, such as the looming oil shortage and growing awareness of the disamenities of motor traffic. These factors will of course be reflected in the evidence given and arguments advanced at inquiries.

of a case before an inspector but public relations and political ballyhoo on a grand scale.

In the Stansted case the Board of Trade (now incorporated into the Department of Trade and Industry) held a non-statutory inquiry (that is, one they were not compelled by law to hold) to consider the objections to the plan. This inquiry illustrated very well the extremely limited value of an inquiry against a determined Ministry and Minister. To put it bluntly the Board of Trade made a hash of presenting its case. The evidence was weak and often contradictory. Counsel for the Board of Trade opened their case by laying down certain conditions which, he said, would have to be met if Stansted were to be the site for London's third airport. As the official witnesses crumbled under cross-examination it became very clear that few of the conditions would be met.

The inspector reported against the proposal. To do otherwise he would have had to stand on his head. But the President of the Board of Trade (Douglas Jay) had no similar inhibitions and stuck to his Ministry's original plan. It was only when Mr Jay had ceased to be President of the Board of Trade—and after an amateur but highly effective public relations campaign by the opponents of the scheme—that Mr Anthony Crosland ordered the establishment of the Roskill Commission to consider the problem. One of the Roskill Commission's first decisions was to rule out Stansted.

The outcome of the Roskill Commission was equally instructive. The Commission (with Professor Sir Colin Buchanan dissenting) favoured the Cublington site. Announcement of its findings was the signal for a massive propaganda effort by the defenders of that part of Buckinghamshire. Their object was to make it politically impossible for the Government to do what the Roskill Commission had recommended it should do and by means of a brilliant but expensive campaign they succeeded.

Cublington and Stansted were *causes célèbres*. What was achieved in these cases, despite the views of Ministers and despite the findings of the most high-powered public inquiry ever held, cannot easily be repeated elsewhere. The defenders of Stansted and Cublington were lucky: they had the support of their county councils; they had a constituency of well-off middle-class people, many of them with professional skills to offer the campaign; by the same token they had money (the Wing Airport Resistance Association spent £3,500 on professional public relations in the last stage of the campaign); they had the established amenity movement on their side in saying that the airport should not be built on an inland site; above all they had an alternative at Foulness, and powerful financial interests supporting its development. The Brent Geese, for whom the Royal Society for the Protection of Birds (in normal circumstances itself a powerful pressure group) pleaded, never had a chance.

The lesson is that the public inquiry should never be treated as the final round in the battle unless, of course, you win it. There are other, broader considerations which can be brought before Ministers; there is perhaps new evidence or a refinement of your alternative. There are MPs who may be persuaded to agree with you in sufficient numbers to make a particular decision politically impossible.

One strength of a pressure group when the public inquiry has closed, and even after the Minister has formally announced a decision, lies in the great power resting with the Minister. The Minister sponsored the plan in the first place. His officials defended it at inquiry. The inspector supported it, and now the Minister has accepted the inspector's recommendation. To say that the Minister is judge and jury in his own cause is grossly unfair, as we have just seen, but that is how he appears to the public at large, to the press and to MPs. Any failure on his part to consider new evidence, the slightest appearance of ministerial arrogance or unwillingness to listen to opponents, is now exploitable by an opposing pressure group.

But the pressure group which seeks to exploit such weaknesses needs to know what it is about. There is no point in sticking pins in a Minister when only spears will do. The Minister's inner strength is that having announced his decision he fears to lose face by going back on it. Pressure at this stage needs to be a neatly balanced compound of criticism of ministerial failings and presentation of new evidence such that 'any fair-minded person, and the Minister is a fair-minded man, must think again'. But don't waste time and money embarking on this type of campaign unless you reckon the political weight you can pull gives you a chance of winning.

This sort of campaign is not the only way to overturn a ministerial decision following public inquiry. There are three other possible 'courts of appeal' which should be carefully considered:

The High Court There is no administrative court in Britain; Ministers defend and justify their policies and decisions to Parliament, not to the courts. But the courts do have a role, not in questioning Ministers' decisions but in ensuring that the rules of natural justice were observed in reaching those decisions, and that Ministers and their servants did not act *ultra vires* (beyond the defined powers they have been granted).

At the end of ministerial decisions following a public inquiry there is usually a note drawing public attention to the fact that application may be made to the High Court within six weeks to have the decision quashed on the grounds that it is not within the power of the Act under which the Minister claims to have acted, or that there has been failure to comply with the procedural requirements in such a way as to disadvantage interested parties.

It is no good going to the High Court because you think the Minister has made the wrong decision, but if you think he reached that decision the wrong way then you may have a case. An example was a planning appeal case in which the Minister of Housing and Local Government refused an appeal but gave as his reason for doing so a danger to traffic which would arise if the development took place. Now, danger to traffic had not been alleged at the public inquiry. The appellants had had no chance to argue that it was untrue or exaggerated or to bring rebutting evidence. The Minister's decision was quashed by the Court.

The Council on Tribunals This is an advisory body charged with supervising the conduct of tribunals of various kinds and of public inquiries. It cannot quash a Minister's decisions, but it can criticize inquiry procedures. For example, the 1970–1 annual report of the Council commented on the Greater London Development Plan inquiry: 'The member of the Council who has visited the GLDP inquiry, while recognizing that the Chairman [of the Inquiry] has been anxious to ensure maximum informality in the proceedings, has observed that the difficulties facing the "small objector" at this type of inquiry are considerable and that the complexity of the proceedings must deter if not intimidate such persons.' The report goes on to express the hope that the Government will review the procedures for future such inquiries. The Council has also commented from time to time on the suitability of appointments of persons as inspectors or assessors at inquiries.

It is most unlikely, if your group finds a fault in the procedure, that it will persuade the Council to condemn the inquiry and urge that the whole exercise be gone through again. It is much more likely that the Council will regret the fault and press the Ministry concerned to ensure that it does not happen again. But the possibility remains that the Council could find that a particular inquiry had been so misconducted that it should be held all over again. If the Council said so then it would be very hard for the Minister concerned to do other than comply.

The Ombudsman (Parliamentary Commissioner for Administration). He is the last—but usually vain—hope of many pressure groups faced with what they think is a hopelessly wrong decision. As his full title implies, he is concerned only with administration and maladministration. The only ground of complaint to the Commissioner (and it must be made via an MP) is that maladministration has occurred. This term is very ill defined. Indeed its definition is only now being built by the Commissioner's own decisions. To date, these have not generally proved helpful to pressure groups. Both ombudsmen who have so far held the post have been former departmental civil servants of great seniority. Not surprisingly they have generally found procedures by other civil servants (they cannot consider local government matters) to be satisfactory.

A typical case was the complaint made by the Ramblers' Association in 1971 to the Ombudsman about the handling by the Minister of Transport and subsequently the Secretary of State for the Environment of the decision on the M 40 motorway route through the Chilterns. The complainants alleged that the alternative route put forward by a number of amenity societies at the public inquiry had not been properly considered. In particular they pointed out that this alternative had never

90

been examined by the Landscape Advisory Committee, which advises the Minister (and now the Secretary of State) on such matters. But the Committee *had* examined the route put forward by the Ministry of Transport and subsequently adopted by Ministers.

The Ombudsman found that the Committee had not examined the alternative route, though they had looked at something similar at an earlier stage. He also found that the Minister of the day had consulted the Committee's chairman who held—contrary to the views of some of his members—that there was no need for the Committee to consider the objectors' alternative. The Commissioner decided that no maladministration had occurred. He may have been right or wrong—it depends what you mean by maladministration—but he left behind a definite sense of grievance among objectors to the official route for the motorway.

The Ombudsman is in much the same position as the Council on Tribunals. He cannot overrule a Minister, but in those few cases where he has stated firmly that a Minister or his officials were wrong the decision has usually been reversed.

The courts of appeal against a ministerial decision are therefore limited in their powers, and not generally willing to seek to extend the limits within which they work. The best court of appeal remains public opinion as interpreted by the media and Parliament.

Inquiry procedure

In the 1950s and early 1960s the rules for procedure before, during and after public inquiries were a major battleground. The issuing of the inspector's report to interested parties and the sending of a full and explanatory decision letter by the Minister concerned only became standard practice after the report of the Franks Committee in 1957. The rules are now more or less clearly set, and the part we are especially concerned with is the inquiry itself.

Whatever the subject of the inquiry the Minister concerned will be required by statute to give notice of the date and place of the inquiry a reasonable time in advance. Make sure that the rules have been observed. A pressure group mounting a case at a public inquiry will need all the time it can get to prepare its case in detail. There are different rules governing procedure at inquiries held under different statutes. There are no rules at all for some types of inquiries. Find what the rules governing your inquiry are by writing to the Ministry organizing it, and then read the rules carefully.

Legal representation

Inquiries have gradually become more formalized. Concern about fair procedures has tended to make Ministries and inspectors follow rules or codes of practice which have a formalizing effect. Secondly, lawyers are much involved in inquiries, and they bring with them the manners and formalities of the courts.

Despite this trend the average inquiry remains a fairly relaxed affair. Inspectors and lawyers will go out of their way to make sure that an individual objector has every chance to put his argument even if he does so at time-wasting length and verbosity. Opposing counsel and their clients will make friendly arrangements to take witnesses in an order convenient to laymen with full-time jobs. Savage or unfair cross-examination is unusual at inquiries, and counter-productive when it happens.

Must your group employ a lawyer and if so what sort of lawyer? Broadly the answer is that in a major inquiry lasting several days or more, when evidence from a number of witnesses must be marshalled, and witnesses (perhaps with technical or professional qualifications) from the other side must be cross-examined, you should be represented by counsel if possible. If you have to do it on the cheap, then a solicitor.

There are, however, a lot of smaller inquiries where legal representation is not necessary. A local amenity society opposing a plan to close a field path certainly does not need a laywer unless some curious point of law is involved. The inquiry will probably be over by lunch time and there will not be more than a handful of witnesses on either side. In a case like this any articulate, clear-headed individual can handle the case. Similarly an amenity society fielding a spokesman at a planning appeal inquiry in support of the local authority does not need a lawyer. In such a case the local authority will be legally represented—probably by a qualified member of its own staff. The pressure group's spokesman can best appear as one of their witnesses.

Briefing counsel must be done properly. The etiquette of the bar demands that laymen can only approach barristers (which is what counsel are) through a solicitor, but you can tell your solicitor of any particular barrister you have in mind. If yours is a planning case remember that there is a vigorous and numerous 'planning bar' whose members specialize in these issues.

A Queen's Counsel is an experienced and successful barrister. He costs more than a 'junior', that is, a barrister who has not yet taken silk (become a QC). A QC will have to be accompanied by a 'junior', and so you have two fees (as well as the solicitor's) to pay. The barrister's fee is a lump sum which is marked on his brief. If the inquiry goes on longer than expected he will have to be paid a 'refresher' each day.

In a 1969 public inquiry concerning a disputed road proposal the services of a QC at the planning bar and his junior were required by the opposing amenity societies for a week. The bills worked out like this: solicitors' fees (for attending meetings, briefing counsel, preparing proofs of evidence—see below and Appendix I) £1,125; counsels' fees £1,500 (QC £1,300, junior £200); charges for copying documents, hotel accommodation, witnesses' expenses, etc. £180—a total of £2,805. But in this case the solicitors made a reduction in their charges of £230, bringing the total bill down to under £2,600.

You are paying good money, so get your money's worth. Take the briefing of counsel seriously and make sure he is given every chance to understand your case. This will mean a series of meetings before the opening of the inquiry, and the group should appoint a small sub-committee with specific responsibility for briefing counsel.

During the inquiry itself there should always be one senior representative of the group present who will sit with counsel and solicitor. A good barrister gets on top of his case—however unfamiliar the subject—very quickly and thoroughly, but this is no substitute for the local and intimate knowledge that the group's officials possess. If the group can find one person to cover the entire inquiry so much the better; failing that a shift system will have to be operated. At an inquiry laymen can and do sit beside their legal representatives, so that it is easy to pass a note to the barrister during cross-examination or to whisper a word of advice or information.

Proofs of evidence

At an inquiry each witness reads out a statement of his views; this is normally written down in advance and is called his proof of evidence. A typical proof is reproduced at Appendix I. Note that it begins by stating the witness's full name and qualifications.

All proofs of evidence should be submitted to counsel in draft form as far in advance of the inquiry as possible. He and the solicitor acting for the group will have advice on the material to be included in each proof and the method of presenting it.

When the proofs have been agreed with the lawyers and with the witnesses they should be typed and duplicated. Double space the typing and type on one side of the paper only; this makes it easy for those using the proofs to make notes on them, and in this form they can also be distributed to the press. You will need enough copies of each proof to hand out at the inquiry to everyone who wants one. It is good public relations to make your case as fully available as possible, and the inspector and opposing counsel will certainly expect to have copies. There are always more people wanting copies than you expect, so allow for this.

The witness gives his evidence by reading out the proof of evidence, which will already have been distributed to others present. If it has not for any reason been distributed the proof should be read at dictation speed. Few inspectors take shorthand.

What happens at an inquiry

At the beginning of the inquiry the inspector takes his seat and introduces himself by giving his name and qualifications and stating the terms of his instructions from the Minister. He then 'takes the appearances', which means that he makes a list of all those who wish to be heard. By custom he takes the major parties to the dispute first. For example, in an inquiry into a motorway plan he will first list the Department of the Environment, followed by the principal objectors. After these and any other obvious big boys (for instance, a local authority) have been listed it becomes something of a free for all, and in a big inquiry it can take an hour or two to get the list completed.

The inspector then usually announces the order in which he intends to take evidence. This does not mean the order of individual spokesmen and witnesses—that has still to be worked out—but the broad categories of evidence. In our hypothetical motorway case he will begin with the opening speech for the Department of the Environment as the planners of the motor-way, followed by their witness or witnesses. Then he will hear any objectors to the entire route. After that he will take objec-tors to different sections of the route, starting from one end. After each witness has given his proof of evidence he may be asked questions by his own counsel, although these are often also interpolated as the witness goes through his evidence. After that he is cross-examined or questioned by other counsel or individuals present who wish to do so. It is very important to realize that any person appearing at the inquiry can put ques-tions to a witness.

Each counsel or spokesman for each party to the inquiry makes an opening speech and then calls his witnesses. They may be subjected to cross-examination and often to re-exam-ination by their own counsel. When all the witnesses for one party have been heard their counsel sums up in a closing speech. As well as objectors represented in this formal way there will often be others who appear by themselves and simply make a statement. They can then themselves be questioned by other parties (or their representatives) at the inquiry.

Beware the device I once saw used by Oxfordshire County Council at a motorway inquiry. They sent one of their legal staff along to support the official proposal. When the counsel for the objectors sought to cross-examine him the county council representative claimed to be present as an advocate and therefore not subject to cross-examination. The inspector allowed this. Evasion of this kind should be publicized im-mediately.

In a long inquiry the sorting out of the proper order of the evidence can be very complicated. The Ministry concerned usually appoints a 'programming officer', who has a desk and a telephone just outside the room or hall where the inquiry is being held. His job is to predict several days in advance when a particular witness is likely to be needed or when the case for a particular group or local authority will come on. He keeps in touch with all these people by telephone and ensures they get to the inquiry at the right time. It is a good rule to make friends with the programme officer. If one of your key witnesses has a vital business meeting on the afternoon when he was to have been called the programme officer can get you out of a jam.

A complication in many inquiries is what lawyers call 'the rights of third parties'. Suppose that the local amenity society, disliking the proposed motorway route, has suggested an alternative. That alternative will itself affect the interests of other individuals and communities, who may wish to be present and object—but there is no statutory procedure for warning them. In practice the sponsors of the official proposal will make sure that third parties are present to support the Ministry case. But this will not necessarily happen in a compulsory purchase order case where the appellant against the order suggests that an alternative site should be bought. The complications may be somewhat relieved by the provision of the Highways Act 1971, which requires objectors to road schemes putting forward alternatives to give notice of these to the Department of the Environment.

Technically a third-party objector may have no right to be heard. In the compulsory purchase order case it could be argued that should the ministerial choice ultimately fall on his property then that proposal too will be subject to inquiry. In practice inspectors bend over backwards to let third parties be heard, and Government avoids writing extra safeguards for them into legislation so as not to slow down still further already cumbersome planning procedures.

Putting your case together
Remember: an inquiry is a means of informing the Minister. The inspector is a man appointed to do that. He will patiently put up with a lot of rhetoric and emotion and irrelevancy, but these things will cut no ice with him. If you are objecting to a proposal he wants to know why and what alternative suggestions, if any, you have to make.

This does not mean that if your case is an emotional one you should try to conceal this. If you are objecting to a plan to build on the best bit of local open space then it is quite reasonable to get emotional about the subsequent deprivation of children and old age pensioners who currently enjoy it. In such a case emotion is relevant.

Just don't overdo it. Every bit of countryside that a new motorway slices through is liable to be described by its defenders as a vital part of England's heritage. Maybe it is. But prove it. How is it designated on the county map? Are there popular footpaths or parking places? Will it spoil an acknowledged panorama from some other point? These are the kind of solid facts about the countryside you are defending that the inspector wants to know. Let your principal witness express the grave and heartfelt concern of the objectors and let the others stick to the facts they are specially able to give.

Organizing the case

In a major public inquiry, organizing and orchestrating the pressure group's case is a sizable task. Think, for instance, of a planning inquiry where the hypothetical problem is the siting of a new switching station required by the Central Electricity Generating Board to switch current out of the grid into local supply lines. The CEGB wish to use a site in a designated area of outstanding natural beauty. The county council as planning authority have reluctantly, and after prolonged consultation with the CEGB about possible alternatives, agreed to this. The local amenity society prefers one of the other sites. Fortunately the Secretary of State has decided, despite the county's view, to 'call in' the application and settle it himself. The amenity society must now plan its case.

What witnesses shall it call? The way to approach this question is not by thinking of names but of aspects of the subject. and of influential bodies which can usefully be represented. Thus the committee might produce a list of possible witnesses:

1. *The group's secretary.* He will state the aims and size of the group, and make a general attack on the choice of the site on the grounds of its importance to local amenity.

2. *Qualified architect/planner.* He will give more expert backing

to what the secretary has said, and will also give evidence about the preferred alternative site.

3. *A retired communications engineer.* He will give evidence of the rapcticability of the alternative site and will also be available to supply advice on cross-examination of the other side's expert witnesses.

The remaining witnesses are chosen to demonstrate the breadth of opposition rather than for their ability to add anything to what the first three have to say.

4. *The Clerk of the Parish Council* for the site objected to.

5. A spokesman for the local branch of the *National Farmers' Union* to state that the land on the CEGB's site is more productive than on the alternative.

6. Local *footpath society* or *Ramblers' Association* representative to say how damaging the loss of the local footpath involved will be to the interests of their members.

Getting this lot organized is much more than simply securing their willingness to give evidence. Their proofs will have to be obtained (very hard work) and edited to ensure they do not overlap too much and do not go on too long. Each witness will need some coaching in the kind of cross-examination he may get. Ideally each witness should also be seen by the group's council before the inquiry, or at least by their solicitor.

And so the inspector will complete the inquiry with the clear impression in his mind of a well-constructed case based on a broad range of objections from the affected communities and individuals. His report to his Minister and perhaps the Minister's decision will reflect this.

8
Whitehall

The theory of Whitehall is simple. Ministers are in charge. Civil servants advise Ministers and do the donkey work of carrying out agreed policies and decisions adopted by Ministers. Ministers in turn are responsible to Parliament. Broadly the theory is true in practice. The big decisions, the ones that govern other decisions for years ahead, are taken by the politicians. The smaller administrative decisions which flow from these are taken by civil servants.

Where the theory breaks down is in its implied assumption of Ministers' freedom. In fact the constraints imposed on a Minister by the Civil Service are very great. How far a Minister can break out of those constraints and take his own decisions against the advice of civil servants is a measure of the strength of his personality and determination.

The Civil Service at the moment is in a state of flux. Until the end of the 1960s the structure of the service was in all essentials that laid down in the Northcote-Trevelyan reforms of the mid-nineteenth century. There were three major classes of civil servants: administrative, executive and clerical. The administrators (usually Oxbridge graduates and the best of their year) had the top jobs. They were the men at the Minister's elbow, who worked out new policies and drafted the white papers. The executives were in the middle. They executed the decisions of the Ministers and administrators. The clericals did the humble pen-pushing.

The Fulton Report of 1968 recommended a sweeping change, and this is now being implemented. The old division between administrators, executives and clerks has been destroyed, and these are all now merged into what is called the General Category. Other civil servants who previously belonged to 'professional' classes have been added to this category, notably economists, statisticians and public relations men (information officers as the Civil Service calls them). The other two main categories are the Science Category and the Professional and Technology Category. The latter includes architects, engineers, surveyors, doctors, accountants, planners and so on.

The Civil Service employs hundreds of professional men in these and other disciplines. Civil Service engineers design the motorways. Doctors advise the Minister in charge of the Health Service. Every department has its lawyers and accountants. Planners and architects have an obvious role in the Department of the Environment.

Pressure groups may come into contact with civil servants in this category from time to time: the engineers, for example, when a motorway is planned; the doctors, if you have a problem about local hospital services. But the category that matters most to pressure groups is the General. It is from this category that most ministerial advisers are drawn, and whose members will have most influence on decisions that matter to a pressure group.

At the very top of the Service there are no categories. There the Service is now said to be 'open'. The Permanent Secretary in charge of the Department of the Environment could in theory be the former Chief Highways Engineer or former head of the economists in the Department. But at present—and no doubt for some time to come—most Permanent Secretaries are ex-members of the old administrative class.

There is now a new division in the Service. Under the old system the bright Oxbridge graduates went into the administrative class and worked their way up it. Except possibly in their earliest jobs they were never at any time subject to direction by the humbler executives or clericals. Now the distinction is between 'fast stream' and 'main stream' civil servants. In theory the bright graduate who fails to shine as expected may be shunted to the main stream and school leavers who are proved outstanding may be switched into the fast stream.

The chart at Appendix J illustrates the career structure in the General Category of the Civil Service and the salaries (in central London) paid to people at each rank.

Study this, because a pressure group needs to know with whom it is dealing. You need to make sure that you are talking to officials at a high enough level to be effective. Note for instance the distinction between a Higher Executive Officer (A) and the humbler main stream man who lacks the magic letter. Note that the Senior Executive Officer and Senior Principals are main stream men. They will not be taking final decisions on anything that matters very much.

The magic rank, so far as a local pressure group is concerned, is Assistant Secretary. Assistant Secretaries have real power. It is a rank not usually reached before the late thirties and often later. It involves taking charge of a major segment of policy implementation and being expected to get on with it with a minimum of informal supervision. A pressure group talking to anyone of lower rank can rarely hope to influence policy.

There is one other middle rank which needs special attention, and that is Principal. Every Minister has what is called a private office, headed by a Private Secretary, who is usually a Principal. The private office is the Minister's personal staff. They feed him papers from the rest of the department. They decide what letters he should see. They listen to his telephone conversations with other civil servants and other Ministers. One reason why the Service is so powerful is that it is extremely difficult for two Ministers to get together to concert plans without their civil servants knowing and maybe alerting other Ministers' civil servants to what is in the wind.

The Private Secretary is usually an Oxbridge graduate (formerly of the administrative class) in his middle or later thirties. He works as Private Secretary to the Minister for eighteen months or two years, and after this spell is automatically promoted to Assistant Secretary. During his stint in the private office he receives a special allowance on top of his normal salary to compensate foɪ the long hours of hard work. If you ever happen to find yourself on the telephone speaking to the Minister's Private Secretary don't suppose you are addressing a glorified shorthand-typist, still less a personal employee of the Minister. You are addressing the single most influential civil servant in the department with the exception of the Permanent Secretary himself.

Working to the Private Secretary are a varying number of

other junior officials in charge of the Minister's engagements and other aspects of his life.

Junior Ministers have their own private offices which function in the same way though on a smaller scale. The Private Secretary in these cases may be of lower rank, for instance, an executive officer who is considered likely to be good enough to switch to the fast stream or an administration trainee getting his first taste of responsibility.

How can a pressure group tell what level of official is dealing with its affairs? The simplest way is to use reference books. *Whitaker's Almanack* normally names all senior civil servants down to and including Assistant Secretaries and also gives the names of Ministers' Private Secretaries. The names are arranged under the various functional divisions of each Ministry. Current salary ranges are also noted. Broadly similar information is given in *Vacher's Parliamentary Companion*, which also lists all peers and MPs, and gives private addresses and telephone numbers for many of them. Under-Secretaries and above may be looked up in *Who's Who*. The *Imperial Calendar* is the guide to the Civil Service and will give the same information down to a lower level in the hierarchy.

You can also gauge with whom you are dealing if you visit his office. Anyone with experience of the Civil Service can tell the rank of an official by looking at the furniture and fittings in his office. Carpets begin at Principal level and Principals usually have a room to themselves. Assistant Secretaries always get rooms to themselves *and* Personal Secretaries. They also have grander furniture—notably a comfortably padded armchair which no doubt marks a subtle transition from doing to thinking. Under-Secretaries have the same style of furniture but bigger offices and curtains at their windows. If you are going any higher the rank of the official you are seeing will have been made amply clear to you in advance of the meeting. At the top the Permanent Secretary has his own private office staff just as the Minister does.

Public relations
The Civil Service possesses a formidable public relations machine. It is as well to know how it works in case you have to match your wits against it.

Each Ministry has its own information division manned by professional public relations men. The head of the division is usually an Assistant Secretary, though in some of the very big departments (Environment and the Treasury) he may be a rung above this. He and his staff advise Ministers on the presentation of their policies and the timing of announcements of new decisions. The head of the information division, if he is any good, is a very close and personal adviser to the Minister.

Information personnel prepare the Ministry's press releases, organize its press conferences, maintain a press office dealing with newspapermen's queries over the telephone and plan its advertising campaigns.

Most of the time Whitehall press offices are too busy with national issues to deal more than cursorily with criticisms from local pressure groups. Indeed they will often not know what a local pressure group is saying until it gets into the national press. One of their blind spots is their general failure to read the local press. In most departments the daily press—national and regional—is read and cut every morning. The cuttings will be on the Minister's desk by mid-morning at the latest. Whether the Minister reads them is another matter. But if a local pressure group wants its publicity noticed in Whitehall it must either get into the daily press or start sending clippings of its news stories direct to the Ministers concerned.

You will come across the information staff of the Ministry if you mount a deputation to see the Minister. Unless the Ministry and its information staff are deeply asleep (and this happens) an information officer will attend the meeting with instructions either to prepare a statement for issue to the press after the meeting or to be ready to make such a statement if it is decided at the meeting or subsequently that one is needed.

Ostensibly the Minister is receiving the deputation simply to hear its views. But Ministers are in politics, and if the policy he is pursuing is counter to that of the deputation, he will probably see it as an opportunity to demonstrate not only his reasonableness in listening to contrary views but the rightness of his own.

Before the meeting breaks up the leader of the deputation, if the Minister does not raise the matter himself, should ask whether it is the department's intention to issue a statement to the press. It has been known for a department to issue a statement without informing the deputation, and thus get coverage for its own views through a one-sided account of the meeting. Remember that the Ministry's information staff can have a statement circulated to every office in Fleet Street (including that of your own regional papers) within a matter of hours, and your chances of catching up with it to give your side of the story are slender.

If the Minister says there is not going to be a press statement don't be awed into thinking that you must not issue one yourself. Unless the whole basis of the meeting has been confidential there is no reason why you shouldn't, but, as a matter of courtesy, tell the Minister that you intend to do so. The official side may then suggest an agreed press statement to be issued by the department, but giving both sides of the case. There is no harm in this except that it is not likely to be a very full-blooded document from the point of view of either side. That may suit the Ministry if they are trying to play the issue down—but it may not suit you. The deputation can always insist on issuing its own statement, but if the meeting has been a useful one and you think that the Ministry is moving your way you may not wish to upset them by doing so.

The advantage of separate statements is that both sides can say exactly what they like and the press can then quote both, but for a deputation attending a meeting in Whitehall away from their home base it may be technically difficult to get a release prepared and distributed within a matter of hours. On the other hand an agreed statement will, after joint drafting, be duplicated in the department's information office and distributed through Government machinery. An agreed statement is what it says it is, that is, both parties have assented to every word of it. The deputation does not have to accept any wording it does not like or which misrepresents in any degree its point of view.

Three points to watch:

1. There will be a headline on the release. Make sure you agree this as well as the text.

2. The release will appear on official paper, so make sure that

in the very first line it is made clear that this is a joint document.

3. At the top of the department's press release paper will be a telephone number for newspapermen to call with any further inquiries about the release. Make sure that a telephone number is included where a spokesman for the group can also be contacted.

Friends or enemies?
It is common platform rhetoric for pressure groups to attack civil servants as faceless men who wield enormous and un-checked power. This may be good for a round of foot-stamping applause at the local protest meeting, but the danger is that too many pressure groups come to believe their own rhetoric and this leads them to wage a misdirected and ineffective campaign.

Civil servants and their bossess are better people to deal with than most. Government in this country now has a respect-able and lengthening tradition of consultation with pressure groups of all sorts. Civil servants expect to receive deputations and to hold meetings to discuss their plans with interested and affected persons. They will normally do this willingly and as a matter of course. You may find a very different attitude if you are up against, for instance, a major industrial concern. There, if consultation is offered at all, it is likely to be a self-conscious piece of public relations window-dressing.

Ministry officials can help you if they are convinced you have a good case. Why spoil your chances by blackguarding them for doing their job?

Distinguish, if you can, between the area of the civil servants' responsibility and that of the politicians. The civil servants will generally be responsible for the details of a plan. In the case, for example, of a new motorway the line of route will have been prepared in detail by the professional civil engineers at the Department of the Environment. The decision to build the motorway at all is a political one and was probably taken years ago by a previous government.

This division of responsibility indicates how you must divide your campaign. If you want to stop the motorway altogether you must tackle the Minister responsible at political level. If you want to shift the route 100 yards your best bet is a reasoned argument put forcefully and with maximum publicity, but also with complete courtesy, to the officials as long in advance of the publication of official proposals as possible.

If the officials you are dealing with do err and treat your representations with contempt or discourtesy then you have been given a strong card to play. This is excellent press and parliamentary material, and you will have no difficulty in getting the matter raised in the House and putting the responsible Minister on the defensive. But play it carefully. The object is not to score points off the Minister (who is probably furious that his officials behaved so ham-fistedly) but to make him change his mind.

The worst charge against the Civil Service is that it behaves in a needlessly secretive way, and in my experience this is true. The Civil Service is a formal organization. It has to be because it is so big. Work proceeds according to carefully planned schedules and well-tried 'drills'. This is exemplified in the procedure for making and publicizing new motorway plans, which have been under increasing public criticism recently.

The Department of the Environment's stand is quite simple. They say there is ample room for public debate on a new motorway plan in their procedures. Once the Department has selected its preferred route this is published as a 'draft order scheme' which is open to objections and which will be, if the objections are at all substantial, subject to public inquiry.

If details of possible routes are made known before that stage, or if the general public is consulted about possibilities, say the Department, then land and homes which may never be affected will be 'blighted' by fear of the scheme, and far more people will be inconvenienced than is necessary.

This is a very typical Civil Service argument. It has two great defects. The first is that it takes insufficient account of human nature, which is curious. It assumes that people can be slotted neatly into a schedule of official procedures. Secondly, it ignores the great advantages to the official proposals which this procedure confers. Although no route is published and individuals and voluntary organizations are not consulted before publication of the draft order, local authorities *are* consulted 'in confidence'. The local councils get an early chance to persuade the Department to adopt a route which they consider satisfactory. The effect is that when that route is published it has the backing not only of the Department but also of the local authorities. The Department then uses the support of the local authority (the elected representatives of local people) to show that the scheme is locally supported. Yet the elected representatives have considered the matter confidentially and without reference to the constituents.

This secrecy is now being broken down. The enterprising *Birmingham Post* has pioneered an almost foolproof method of predicting motorway routes well in advance of official publication. They send out a reporter to plot the line of test drillings made by the highway engineers. More recently the Waltham Holy Cross Urban District Council in Essex has deliberately broken confidentiality about a motorway scheme— to the Department's intense annoyance.

It seems certain that within the near future the procedures now followed will be radically revised in the direction of a much more prolonged and open debate. This tendency will be further assisted by the fact that more pressure groups are now opposing new motorway schemes in principle, instead of confining themselves to criticism of a particular route. *

To be fair to the Department, there are cases in which this sort of open discussion has taken place. The M 40 route over the Chilterns (discussed in another context in Chapter 5) was one. Ministry of Transport officials met amenity societies to discuss possible routes three years before a draft scheme was published and nearly four years before a public inquiry was held. Possible routes were widely canvassed in the journals and newsletters of various organizations throughout that period, and although the alternative proposals pressed by the amenity societies affected more homes than the officials' preferred scheme, no complaints of 'blight' were noticed.

This discussion of how motorway proposals are handled

* Since this was written, the DOE has, as anticipated, introduced a new consultation stage whereby the public are given the opportunity to comment on possible alternative routes before the Department publishes its own firm proposals. This consultation is non-statutory, i.e. it may be withdrawn at any time or refused in any particular case.

serves to highlight the Civil Service's principal weakness—a love of secrecy until it is ready to go through its own carefully worked-out consultation procedures. Secrecy—like failure to consult—is your weapon. Don't hesitate to use it. Accusations of secrecy against government departments are always good copy for the press and, adroitly handled, should enable a pressure group to flush out the information it wants before the officials have tied the rest of the potential opposition to their chariot.

9
Pressure and Parliament

Members of Parliament exist to help pressure groups. Never be hesitant about using them.

Your own MP
This is the member with whom most pressure groups invariably have to do. He will help if he can. The 'if' arises when your campaign cuts across the interests of others of his constituents, or when it runs flatly and obviously counter to the policy of his party.

The MP whose constituents are bitterly divided about the route of the new motorway is not likely to come down on one side or the other, unless he knows that his political supporters are concentrated in one camp. He will sit on the fence and say how important it is that the facts should be made fully known at a public inquiry so that the Secretary of State can come to the right decision. But even an MP in this unfortunate position will be as helpful as he can. He can use contacts with Ministers and question time to press for information about official plans. Most MPs will willingly do so.

Contacting your own Member is easy. He almost certainly holds a regular meeting with constituents to discuss their problems (his 'surgery') and this is probably advertised in the local press. If not a telephone call to local party HQ will give you the information. On a major issue, get in quick and get in first. Don't wait to grab five minutes in a crowded surgery session with perhaps a dozen others waiting to be seen. Get at the man at the time and in the circumstances where you can most effectively persuade him into agreeing with you.

MPs are only human. They have sensitive political antennae,

but it is certainly not impossible to persuade an MP to opt for your side in an argument before the others have got a look in. He may regret it later, but if he has backed you and backed you publicly he will find it hard to wriggle out.

Think about your MP's politics. The importance of being non-political was stressed in Chapter 1. It holds good. But if the MP thinks that your pressure group is run by people who will vote for him it is more likely he will give you his unreserved backing. So if you are going to see your Conservative MP and the group's chairman is a long-haired twenty-five-year-old who normally wears flared trousers and a sweater with 'Fuzz Are Pigs' written all over it, don't take him along. Or tell him to wear a suit. Horses for courses is a good rule in pressure-group politics.

Raising it in the House
There are two principal ways in which an MP can raise a local issue in the House of Commons. He can ask the appropriate Minister about it at question time or he can 'raise it on the adjournment'.

Question time is a very overrated institution. In classic constitutional theory it is the moment when Ministers must stand up and defend their policies and actions with no holds barred. It rarely works out that way.

First of all the questioning MP must try to put down on the order paper a question that will be answered orally. If he fails to do that he has no chance to put the all important supplementary questions. And his chances are limited because he is only one of 600-odd MPs, many of whom are seeking to question a Minister on the day allotted to him for questions.

The question itself is known in advance, so the Minister's civil servants have time to prepare a reply for him. But they can only guess (usually very shrewdly) at what the supplementary will be.

But parliamentary questions (PQs in the trade) have their value. They are often the first signal to a Minister and his civil servants that anyone besides a few local cranks is taking an interest in a particular issue. They are also a means of obtaining information, and this goes for those questions which receive only a written answer, but are printed in Hansard.

Sometimes a member on receiving a reply from a Minister will say that he is so dissatisfied that he will seek to 'raise it later on the adjournment'. An adjournment debate is a short debate, usually half an hour or so, in which an MP raises a matter of special concern to him, frequently an issue affecting only his own constituency. The MP concerned opens the debate and a Minister—usually a junior Minister—is present to reply. Between their two speeches there may be time for a couple of other members to contribute briefly, but that will be all. The debate does enable a full exposition of the case to be given but, as with questions, no member can be sure of securing an adjournment debate since there is always competition for the time available. Indeed there are usually very few members present apart from the two or three who may be directly interested. It is simply a means of airing concern and compelling a ministerial response.

Deputations

Another important way in which a member can help a pressure group is by arranging for them to meet a Minister and put their case direct to him. An MP is often prepared to do this on behalf of a group of constituents even if he does not personally support their campaign.

It is possible for pressure groups to see Ministers or civil servants without the aid of MPs, and among national organizations it happens all the time. But Ministers are naturally more reluctant to find time for a small local body, and often the help of an MP or MPs will do the trick.

Advice on how to get the maximum publicity value from a deputation to a Minister is given in Chapter 8.

Which MPs?

A pressure group aiming to make its cause a national issue will need the support of more MPs (and peers) than its own constituency member. A national publicity campaign, if this is developed, will help to attract this support. The group's own MP, if he is backing their case, will drum up more supporters. But the group should be doing this itself by approaching other members likely to be interested in its case. The problem is how to know which MPs will be interested.

111

Nearly every MP has one or two favourite subjects in which he is something of a specialist. They may be subjects which arise naturally from his political or professional background. Thus an MP sponsored by a trade union will probably take a particularly active part in issues affecting its members. An ex-journalist may well be especially concerned about matters affecting the freedom of the press. A landowner will have something to say on farming matters, and so on.

Not all MPs' interests are so obvious. A good example is Mr Arthur Blenkinsop, the Labour MP for South Shields. He is one of his party's acknowledged experts on local government and he is an active member of the Town and Country Planning Association. If you look him up in *Who's Who* you will see that he lists walking as one of his recreations. From this interest springs the work he has done in Parliament on behalf of pressure groups concerned with the protection of National Parks and the countryside generally. He serves as Vice-President of the Ramblers' Association and is a member of the Executive Committee of the National Trust. During the debates on the Local Government Act in 1972, as well as speaking for his party on a wide range of issues covered by the legislation, he led those MPs who wished to see the Government provide strong and independent administration for the National Parks.

A similar example on the other side of the House is Mr Patrick Cormack, the Conservative member for Cannock. He joined Mr Blenkinsop in questioning the Government's National Parks policy. His entry in *Who's Who* shows that one of his recreations is 'visiting old churches', and this has led to his playing an active part in promoting measures to protect churches which have become redundant. Allied with this interest was the considerable part he played during the debates on the Local Government Act in examining the provisions of the legislation for the management of conservation areas.

There is no simple method by which a local pressure group, building its own political contacts for the first time, can discover which MPs have these interests. If you have the personnel and the time available it is an excellent idea to set someone to go through all the entries for MPs in *Who's Who*, and list those who have any official position or recreational interest connected with your cause.

A useful reference work is *Who Does What in Parliament?* by H. Mitchell and P. Birt (1970; obtainable from the authors at 2 Cornwall Mansions, Kensington Court, London W8, at 60p including postage). Messrs Mitchell and Birt are members of the staff of the Parliamentary Labour Party, and their reference book is expert and authoritative. In it they list all the various 'interest groups' into which members are organized. Some of these groups cut across party lines. An example is the recently formed Conservation Group which includes MPs and peers of all parties. Others are grouped within parties. Thus the Parliamentary Labour Party possesses a Forestry Sub-Committee, whose work is perhaps typical of such bodies. Its members meet fairly regularly in order to inform themselves on current forestry issues. They have regular contacts with the Forestry Commission and the private timber-growing industry. In this way—and there are similarly concerned members on the other side of the House—the industry has a readily available panel of spokesmen to probe Government policy.

Mitchell and Birt give the names of the officers of each of these groups. On the Labour side of the House membership of the groups is formalized, and the names of members of any of these groups can be obtained by writing to the Parliamentary Labour Party at the House of Commons (address letters to Mr F. Barlow). On the Conservative side the groups have officers but no formalized membership. Inquiries of Conservative Party officials suggest that these officers, or the Conservative Party organization in the House, would sometimes be prepared to name members especially interested in a subject to outsiders, but not necessarily so.

Other useful works of reference are *The Business Background of Members of Parliament* (1972) and *MPs' Chart* (1971). These are both published by Parliamentary Profiles (194 Palace Chambers, Bridge Street, London SW1) at £3.00 and £1.20 respectively. *Lord on the Board* (1972) £3.60 from the same publisher, deals with the business affiliations of peers. The author of these volumes is Mr Andrew Roth. But there is really no substitute for long hours in the public library with *Who's Who* and back volumes of *Hansard* checking which members are interested in what.

Having found out which MPs are potential allies the pressure group must consider carefully how to approach them. MPs receive vast quantities of unsolicited mail and are adept at using waste-paper baskets. It is extremely unlikely that a circular document about a local issue remote from his own constituency will even be read by an MP. If you want to engage his support you must write a personal letter, and this must begin by referring to the member's interest in the subject. If you decide there are forty MPs worth tackling then you must write (type) forty separate letters: no carbons or duplicating, please.

MPs who do show an interest in your campaign must be kept informed and up to date. If your group produces a news-letter, see that it goes to friendly MPs. Send them copies of your press releases or any propaganda material you produce. Clip a compliments slip with a signature on it to each document. It will remind the MP that there are real people behind the campaign, with whom he has had previous contact.

The House of Lords
Never ignore or underestimate the House of Lords. It contains some of the most influential and formidable spokesmen of pressure groups in the country. Its members are far less subject to party influences than are MPs; its time-tables are more lax and more leisurely; it contains experts on every subject under the sun. Finding out which peers are interested in what and approaching those who may support you is the same process as for the Commons.

The same sorts of procedures are open to peers wishing to raise particular matters. Questions are fewer and usually less pugnaciously put. The Lords' equivalent of the adjournment debate—known in the Upper House as an 'unstarred question' —is a powerful weapon in skilled hands. A good example of its use on behalf of pressure groups (in this case national ones) occurred in February 1972, when Lord Henley, a Liberal peer, put down an unstarred question on the administration of National Parks. In the debate which followed peers of all parties supported Lord Henley. The Government spokesman had come to the House armed with a major new financial concession to the National Parks; even so he was twice on the ropes, once when he did not know if the Government's Countryside Commission had endorsed a particular line of policy or not, and again when he could not explain why the Government was pursuing one policy for two National Parks and another for the other eight.

It is doubtful if such a powerful demonstration of weaknesses and contradictions of Government policy could have been secured in the Commons. Several of the peers taking part were personally experienced in the subject. Lady Wootton, for example, had served as chairman of the National Parks Commission. Lord Foot was a member of the Dartmoor National Park Planning Committee. Lord Henley himself was prominently associated with the National Parks Day campaign mounted by a group of national amenity societies. Lord Kennet was then chairman of the Council for the Protection of Rural England.

Lobbying

The processes described above are known collectively as 'lobbying'. Lobbying is quite a sizable business in this country. Nearly all national organizations whose interests and members are affected by government actions lobby MPs and peers from time to time.

The system is well described in *British Pressure Groups* by J. D. Stewart (Oxford University Press, 1958). Stewart deals with the national lobbies, but there is no fundamental difference for a local organization except that it has to go into action with less money, less experience and often at short notice.

The techniques employed by permanent national lobbyists may be very elaborate. Public relations firms are frequently employed to put a particular case to MPs. Glossy propaganda literature is lavishly distributed. Receptions and parties are organized, at which it is hoped to influence MPs' minds. Members are found to act as the spokesmen of a cause or campaign.

How far such methods make any difference to what Ministers and Parliament ultimately decide is almost impossible to judge. But almost any MP will tell you that there is one tried and tested method of lobbying which does work—and that is the constituents' letter. A member who receives a dozen or so letters from his constituents on a given issue will take notice.

If it is a local issue he will take a great deal of notice. Thus MPs of all parties have fought to maintain local railway lines in their constituencies in face of government policy to close these down. By the same token an MP who normally defends the conservation of National Parks will be willing to back the creation of a new industrial eyesore in one if it helps the employment prospects of his constituents.

Petitions

Petitioning Parliament tends to be one of the first exercises a newly formed pressure group thinks of. It is not a bad idea provided you know why you are doing it and what you hope to get out of it. A petition is not going to win you your case. Eric Taylor in his useful book *The House of Commons at Work* (reprinted 1971; Pelican, 35p) comments: 'In fact public petitions, except when part of a carefully organized parliamentary campaign, appear to be little but a waste of money and energy on the part of the petitioners. . . .'

This is true as far as it goes, but ignores the publicity value of a petition to the organizers in the locality where the signatures are gathered. A pressure group may well spend several months over the gathering of signatures, and *each week* there will be a report in the local paper saying how many signatures have so far been gathered.

But unless your petition is to end in the ignominy of being found to be not in order, make sure that you follow the rules. You can get these by writing to the Clerk to the Committee on Public Petitions at the House of Commons. Eric Taylor gives the substance of the rules as follows:

1. A petition must be addressed to 'the Honourable the Commons of Great Britain and Northern Ireland in Parliament assembled'.

2. It must be respectful and decorous, especially in the references to Parliament and the courts of justice.

3. It must pray for something—i.e. it must be couched in the form of a prayer, not in terms of a demand or an exhortation.

4. It must not ask for a grant of public money, or refer to

debates in either House or to motions on the Order Book of the House.

5. The top sheet of the petition must be written by hand: at least one signature must appear on the same page as the handwritten prayer of the petition: if other sheets are added for additional signatures they must be headed with the prayer of the petition (which may, in this case, be printed).

6. The petition must contain no erasures or interlineations.

The petition has to be presented by a particular member. He may, if he notifies the Speaker in advance, state the 'material allegations' contained in the petition when presenting it. There will be no debate. The majority of petitions are presented in silence.

Private Bills

There is another sort of parliamentary petition, and that is the petition against a private Bill. Pressure groups sometimes have to deal with these. Private Bills are the means by which various statutory bodies obtain parliamentary authority to undertake certain activities. At the time of writing this book the Central Electricity Generating Board is promoting a private Bill to enable it to build new hydro-electric installations in Snowdonia.

The essence of a private Bill is that it is promoted by a single body for its own benefit. It is entirely different from a private member's Bill, which is legislation of general public concern promoted by an individual MP.

Opposing a private Bill can be difficult and expensive. The cheapest method is to get it thrown out by the House before it goes to the Opposed Bills Committee. To do this you must find a member or members who are prepared to cry 'Object' when the Bill comes up for second reading. Alternatively he may block the Bill by moving that it be read 'upon this day six months'. The Chairman of Ways and Means who watches over private legislation takes note that a private Bill is being held up in this way, and eventually arranges for it to be debated on the floor of the House.

This is the pressure group's opportunity. If they can muster

117

enough support to throw out the Bill, then the alternative and expensive method of defeating it can be dispensed with. Some of the most famous of these battles in recent years have taken place on proposals for new reservoirs, and local pressure groups such as the Dartmoor Preservation Association and local branches of the National Farmers' Union, the Ramblers' Association and so on have been very much involved. Usually such Bills are passed at second reading if only because many members feel that legislation promoted by a public authority such as a water board should be fully examined in committee, but it is not unknown for the opponents to succeed.

Once through its second reading an opposed private Bill goes before a select committee. Here the procedure is more like that of a court of law than a committee of Parliament. Both sides are represented by counsel, and there are usually a mass of expert witnesses on either side. The proceedings are lengthy and expensive. For instance, it cost the various amenity societies headed by the Dartmoor Preservation Association, which opposed the Plymouth and South West Devon Water Bill in 1971, more than £5,000 in fees to parliamentary agents (firms of solicitors who specialize in parliamentary work) and counsel. And in this case the Committee threw out the Bill after hearing only the promoters' case, barely half way through the expected length of the proceedings.

If your group is ever involved in such a procedure you will find the advice given in Chapter 7 (on Public Inquiries) useful in marshalling witnesses and preparing their evidence.

Bills accepted by the Committee are reported to the House with any amendments, and there is then an opportunity for further amendment or rejection.

A point to watch is the standing of your organization if it wishes to petition against a private Bill. A group set up specifically for this purpose will probably not be allowed to petition. Parliament prefers to deal with bodies of some standing, and which possess a clearly defined local interest affected by the Bill.

In a recent dispute two organizations petitioned against a Bournemouth Corporation Bill enabling the Corporation to take over and develop land regarded by some local residents as public open space. An amenity society established to oppose the plan was refused permission to petition. An existing branch of the Ramblers' Association, established in the area for some years, was allowed to petition.

If a private Bill is not opposed by petition it goes to the Unopposed Bills Committee, where it nevertheless receives thorough scrutiny. Here there is an opportunity for pressure groups to secure minor changes. The method is to ask a friendly MP to get one of his colleagues on the Committee to raise the point giving concern.

Appendices

Appendix A
Public meeting check list

Before the meeting

1. Set out chairs and distribute agenda, if used.

2. Arrange press table (at the front, at an angle of 45° to platform) firm enough for writing on and labelled PRESS: place on it hand-outs of speeches if prepared.

3. Make sure public address equipment is working if required.

4. Put carafe of water and glasses on platform table.

5. Ensure literature stall is organized and manned at rear.

6. If stewards are needed either to show people where to sit or as a safeguard against disorder, make sure they are in position and know their job.

During the meeting

1. Circulate attendance list with space for names and addresses to be entered.

2. Remind chairman half an hour before time at which hire of hall is up.

After the meeting

1. If funds are needed station cash collectors at exits.

2. See, thank and tip caretaker (you may want to come again).

Appendix B
Model constitution for civic societies

This text has been prepared by the Civic Trust. An information sheet is issued by the Trust (17 Carlton House Terrace, London SW1 5AW) giving helpful explanatory notes and advice:

1. **Name**   The name of the Society shall be the ⸺⸺⸺⸺⸺⸺⸺

2. **Objects**   The Society is established for the public benefit for the following purposes in the area comprising⸺⸺⸺⸺⸺⸺ which area shall hereinafter be referred to as 'the area of benefit'.

   a To stimulate public interest in the area of benefit.
   b To promote high standards of planning and architecture in the area of benefit.
   c To secure the preservation, protection, development and improvement of features of historic or public interest in the area of benefit.

   In furtherance of the said purposes but not otherwise the Society through its Executive Committee shall have the following powers:

   i To promote research into subjects directly connected with the objects of the Society and to publish the results of any such research.
   ii To act as a co-ordinating body and to co-operate with the local authority, planning committees, sanitary, drainage and all other local and statutory authorities, voluntary organizations, charities and persons having aims similar to those of the Society.

iii To promote or assist in promoting activities of a charitable nature throughout the area of benefit.

iv To publish papers, reports and other literature.

v To make surveys and prepare maps and plans and collect information in relation to any place, erection or building of beauty or historic interest within the area of benefit.

vi To hold meetings, lectures and exhibitions.

vii To educate public opinion and to give advice and information.

viii To raise funds and to invite and receive contributions from any person or persons whatsoever by way of subscription, donation and otherwise; provided that the Society shall not undertake any permanent trading activities in raising funds for its primary purposes.

ix To take and accept any gifts of property, whether subject to any special trusts or not.

x To sell, let, mortgage, dispose of or turn to account all or any of the property or funds of the Society as shall be necessary.

xi To borrow or raise money for the purposes of the Society on such terms and on such security as the Executive Committee shall think fit, but so that the liability of individual members of the Society shall in no case extend beyond the amount of their respective annual subscriptions.

xii To do all such other things as are necessary for the attainment of the said purposes.

3. **Membership** Membership shall be open to all who are interested in actively furthering the purposes of the Society. No member shall have power to vote at any meeting of the Society if his subscription is in arrears at the time. Junior members shall be those aged less than 18 years at the time their subscription is due; and they shall not be entitled to vote at any meeting of the Society. The subscription of a member joining the Society in the three months preceding ....in any year shall be regarded as covering............ membership for the Society's year commencing on........................ following the date of joining the Society.

125

4. Subscriptions   The annual subscription shall be:

Life members   £..

(The joint life subscription of a married couple shall
be   £..)

Full members   £..

(The joint annual subscription for full membership for
a married couple shall be   £..)

Junior members   £..

or such other reasonable sum as the Executive Committee
shall determine from time to time, and it shall be payable
on or before..each year. Membership shall
lapse if the subscription is unpaid three months after it
is due.

5. Meetings   An Annual General Meeting shall be held in or
about..of each year to receive the
Executive Committee's report and audited accounts and to
elect Officers and Members of the Committee. The Committee shall decide when ordinary meetings of the Society
shall be held and shall give at least..days' notice
of such meetings to all members.

Special General Meetings of the Society shall be held at the
written request of members representing not less than 10
per cent of the existing membership of the Society and whose
subscriptions are fully paid-up. ....members
personally present shall constitute a quorum for a Meeting
of the Society.

6. Officers   Nominations for the election of Officers shall be
made at least 14 days before the Annual General Meeting.
Such nominations shall be supported by a seconder, and
the consent of the proposed nominee must first have been
obtained. The election of Officers shall be completed prior
to the election of further Committee members.

The Officers of the Society shall consist of:

| Chairman | Honorary Secretary |
| (Vice-Chairman) | Honorary Treasurer |

all of whom shall relinquish their office every year and shall be eligible for re-election at the Annual General Meeting. A President and Vice-Presidents may also be elected at a General Meeting of the Society, for periods to be decided at such a meeting. The Executive Committee shall have the power to fill casual vacancies occurring among the Officers of the Society.

7. **The Executive Committee** The Executive Committee shall be responsible for the management and administration of the Society. The Executive Committee shall consist of the Officers and not more than................other members. The Committee shall have power to co-opt further members (who shall attend in an advisory and non-voting capacity). The Officers and members of the Committee shall normally be resident or work in the area of benefit but the Committee shall have power to co-opt additional members from outside the area of benefit. The President and Vice-Presidents may attend any meeting of the Executive Committee but shall not vote at any such meeting. In the event of an equality in the votes cast, the Chairman shall have a second or casting vote. Nominations for election to the Executive Committee shall be made in writing at least 14 days before the Annual General Meeting. They must be supported by a seconder and the consent of the proposed nominee must first have been obtained. If the nominations exceed the number of vacancies, a ballot shall take place in such manner as shall be determined. Members of the Executive Committee shall be elected annually at the Annual General Meeting of the Society. Outgoing members may be re-elected. The Executive Committee shall meet not less than six times a year at intervals of not more than two months and the Honorary Secretary shall give all members not less than seven days' notice of each meeting.

The quorum shall, as near as may be, comprise one third of the members of the Executive Committee.

8. **Sub-committees** The Executive Committee may constitute such sub-committees from time to time as shall be considered necessary for such purposes as shall be thought fit. The Chairman and Secretary of each sub-committee shall be appointed by the Executive Committee and all actions and proceedings of each sub-committee shall be reported to and be confirmed by the Executive Committee as soon as possible. Members of the Executive Committee may be members of any sub-committee and membership of a sub-committee shall be no bar to appointment to membership of the Executive Committee. Sub-committees shall be subordinate to the Executive Committee and may be regulated or dissolved by the Executive Committee.

9. **Expenses of Administration and Application of Funds** The Executive Committee shall, out of the funds of the Society, pay all proper expenses of administration and management of the Society. After the payment of the administration and management expenses and the setting aside to reserve of such sums as may be deemed expedient, the remaining funds of the Society shall be applied by the Executive Committee in furtherance of the purposes of the Society.

10. **Investment** All monies at any time belonging to the Society and not required for immediate application for its purposes shall be invested by the Executive Committee in or upon such investments securities or property as it may think fit, subject nevertheless to such authority, approval or consent whether by the Charity Commissioners or the Secretary of State for Education and Science as may for the time being be required by law or by the special trusts affecting any property in the hands of the Executive Committee.

11. **Trustees** Any freehold and leasehold property acquired by the Society shall and if the Executive Committee so directs any other property belonging to the Society may be vested in trustees who shall deal with such property as the Executive Committee may from time to time direct. Any trustees shall be at least three in number or a trust corporation. The power of appointment of new trustees shall be vested in

the Executive Committee. A trustee need not be a member of the Society but no person whose membership lapses by virtue of paragraph 3 hereof shall thereafter be qualified to act as a trustee unless and until re-appointed as such by the Excutive Committee. The Honorary Secretary shall from time to time notify the trustees in writing of any amendment hereto and the trustees shall not be bound by any such amendments in their duties as trustees unless such notice has been given. The Society shall be bound to indemnify the trustees in their duties (including the proper charge of a trustee being a trust corporation) and liability under such indemnity shall be a proper administrative expense.

12. **Amendments**   This Constitution may be amended by a two-thirds majority of members present at an Annual General Meeting or Special General Meeting of the Society, provided that 28 days' notice of the proposed amendment has been given to all members, and provided that nothing herein contained shall authorize any amendment the effect of which would be to cause the Society at any time to cease to be a charity in law.

13. **Notices**   Any notice required to be given by these Rules shall be deemed to be duly given if left at or sent by prepaid post addressed to the address of that member last notified to the Secretary.

14. **Dissolution**   The Society may be dissolved by a two-thirds majority of members voting at an Annual General Meeting or Special General Meeting of the Society confirmed by a simple majority of members voting at a future Special General Meeting held not less than 14 days after the previous Meeting. If a motion for the dissolution of the Society is to be proposed at an Annual General Meeting or a Special General Meeting this motion shall be referred to specifically when notice of the Meeting is given. In the event of the dissolution of the Society the available funds of the Society shall be transferred to such one or more charitable institutions having objects similar or reasonably similar to those

hereinbefore declared as shall be chosen by the Executive Committee and approved by the Meeting of the Society at which the decision to dissolve the Society is confirmed. On dissolution the minute books and other records of the Society shall be deposited with the Civic Trust.

The permission of the Civic Trust to reproduce this model constitution is gratefully acknowledged.

Appendix C
Model of press release

For immediate release [date]

HUNDREDS WILL SUFFER, SAY EAST BARSET RAIL DEFENDERS

'Immense hardship will be caused to hundreds of people if the East Barset railway line is closed as British Rail intend,' said Mr John Smith, Chairman of the East Barset Public Transport Association yesterday (Wednesday).

Mr Smith was commenting on the results of a census of users of the line taken last Saturday. The line links the villages of Hogglestock, Framley and Plumstead with the city of Barchester, and Barchester with the main line to Paddington at Silverbridge.

Teams of volunteer members of the Association counted passengers joining and leaving trains at Barchester Station and the other stations throughout the day.

Summarizing the results of the census Mr Smith said: 'During Saturday eight trains came into Barchester from the outlying villages and they carried a total of 542 passengers. Trains from Barchester to Silverbridge carried 289.

'Trains from Barchester to the villages carried 490 people while those arriving at Barchester from the Silverbridge direction carried 325.

'The largest numbers joining and alighting at other stations were at Silverbridge and Hogglestock.

'These figures make total nonsense of British Rail's claim that the line is lightly used.'

British Rail in their proposal for closure of the line have

131

stated that buses can carry the passengers displaced from the trains.

Mr Smith said: 'The train from Barchester to Hogglestock takes 25 minutes. The East Barset Road Car Company service takes one hour and five minutes. This includes two diversions from the main road to serve the outlying villages of West Plumstead and Little Hogglestock.

'But we estimate that a direct service would still take nearly twice as long as the train because neither of these villages is more than a quarter of a mile from the main road.'

The Association has further census plans. Future passenger counts will be made on week-days to check on the numbers of people using the trains to come to work or shop in Barchester.

Full details of the census so far are attached (see table of figures).

(*Signed*) P. H. JAMESON
Press Officer

Note to editors: For further queries about this, telephone Mr Smith at Plumstead 032 (home) or Barchester 25798 ext. 41 (office).

Appendix D
Glossary of newspaper terms

Agency   An organization providing news to any paper paying for the service. The most famous is Reuters, but there are many local news agencies covering particular districts.

Bold   Heavy black type.

By-line   The line naming the writer of an article.

Cap.   Capital letter.

Caption   The words printed beneath or alongside a picture.

Close copy   The time at which no further material can be received by the compositors.

Colour   Descriptive writing (as opposed to straight news reporting).

Comps   (Compositors). The men who put together the type for the paper.

Copy   1. Any written or typed material intended to be printed.
               2. The department of a newspaper in which copy is received by dictation over the telephone.

Copy date   The day by which copy must be received at the paper's offices.

Cross-head   A minor heading usually in the centre of column of type. It is inserted for typographical effect only.

Deadline   The time by which a reporter must have his copy ready.

District man   A reporter covering a particular geographical area.

Feature   Descriptive or opinion article (as opposed to news).

Free lance   A newspaperman who sells stories to different papers and is not wholly employed by any one.

Fudge   The stop press column.

Hard   Well-authenticated.

Heavies   Serious newspapers (e.g. *The Times*).

Intro   The first paragraph of a story.

Kill   To decide not to use a story.

Lower case   Small, as opposed to capital, letters.

Nose   The news point on which it is decided to begin a story, e.g. 'Nose it on the blonde . . .'.

Par.   Paragraph.

Piece   Any editorial contribution to the paper.

Point   A measure of type size. The text of this book is printed in 10 point.

Put to bed   Complete editorial work on the paper and send it finally for printing; e.g. 'We go to bed Wednesday night'.

Re-jig   To revise a story extensively, but not to re-write it entirely.

Shoulder   A sub-heading set to the left in column of type.

Slip   A special edition of the paper carrying news for a particular area which will not be of interest elsewhere.

Spike   To throw away (copy). From the spike on the editor's or sub-editor's desk on which unwanted copy is impaled.

Splash   The main front page story.

Spread   A combination of stories and pictures on related

themes on one page or facing pages. Especially the centre spread, used to describe the facing pages in the middle of the paper.

Stone The heavy metal table on which the pages set in type are finally revised before printing.

Story News report.

Streamer A headline running the full width of the page.

Stringer A reporter working for a local paper who provides copy for a paper elsewhere. An experienced reporter on your local weekly may well string for a Fleet Street paper.

Sub (Sub-editor). A journalist who prepares reporters' copy for the printer, cutting it to the length required, checking facts and spelling and marking layout instructions. Also as a verb, 'to sub'.

Tape The teleprinter bringing news stories from main agencies to a newspaper office.

Telephone reporter Typist who types story dictated to him over the 'phone and received through headphones.

Type face Style of type.

Upper case Capital letters.

Appendix E
Model of press notice

Press Notice
2nd September 1972

To:
News Editors
Picture Editors

RAIL PROTESTERS PLAN
PLUMSTEAD STATION DEMO

The East Barset Public Transport Defence Association will demonstrate at the disused Plumstead railway station, starting at 2.30 pm on Saturday 9th September.

YOU ARE CORDIALLY INVITED TO BE REPRESENTED

Announcing the demonstration, the Association's chairman, Mr James Fenton, said: 'We want Plumstead Station reopened. Its continued disuse symbolizes British Rail's negative attitude to the Barchester branch line.

'Since Plumstead Station was closed in 1965 new housing estates with a total population of 3,500 people have been built within a half-mile radius of the station. The majority of working people on these estates have jobs in Barchester.

'At present these people either travel to Barchester by car, adding to the congestion on the city's medieval street system, or they take the bus. The bus journey from Plumstead to the centre of Barchester takes three quarters of an hour, compared to 13 minutes on the train.

'Meanwhile the threat of closure still hangs over the whole

136

Barchester branch on the grounds that it does not pay; yet there are hundreds of passengers waiting to be collected.'

Time-table

2.30 pm. Participants assemble at station and mass on platform.

3.10 pm. Train to Barchester passes. Participants will display posters saying 'STOP', 'PICK UP AT PLUMSTEAD' and 'SAVE THE LINE'.

It is expected that supporters travelling on the train will acknowledge the demonstration as they go through.

Photographs and films The Association has ascertained that the footbridge across the line at the station is still in a safe condition. It is suggested that this will provide the best vantage point for shots of the whole demonstration.

Safety Marshals from the Association will rope off the platform so that persons cannot get within one foot of the edge. Children unaccompanied by adults will not be allowed to take part.

British Rail At the time of preparing this press notice the attitude of British Rail to the demonstration is not clear. It seems unlikely, however, that they will do more than see that no damage is done to their property. In this they will have the full co-operation of the Association's officials and members.

(*Signed*) J. WESTLEY
Press Officer

Note to Editors: I shall be at Plumstead Station from 1.30 onwards on 9th September and available to answer questions or give press representatives any help I can.

Comment

This press notice does two jobs:

1. It informs the media several days in advance of an event which they will want to cover.

2. It provides (through the Chairman's quoted remarks) advance copy which the press can use in advance of the

137

event, thus helping to ensure that a good crowd turns up to the demonstration on the day. Note the detailed advice about times and photographic vantage points given, and the paragraph about safety intended to spike the guns of any reporter who might think there was a story in the 'irresponsibility' of the demonstrators.

Appendix F
Reproduced by permission of the Ramblers' Association.

MAKING £1 DO THE WORK OF £1.64
by WALLY SMITH*

THERE ARE 2,300 members of the Ramb- lers' Association whom I am even more fond of than all the other 20,000 odd put together. They are the ones who covenant their subscriptions.

Each member who covenants his sub- scription still only pays £1 a year. But to the R.A. his £1 is worth £1.64.

Why do so few do it? I suspect because many members are afraid that the process is complicated or expensive. It is neither.

The principle of covenanting is this. A covenant is a legal agreement to give a fixed sum of money, annually for not less than seven years, out of your taxed income to a charity accepted by the Charity Commissioners and the Inland Revenue. And on this sum the tax applicable at the normal rate can be claimed back from the Inland Revenue by the charity concerned. The R.A. is a recognised charity. So, at the present rates of tax, on a £1 sub- scription *paid under covenant*, the R.A. gets from the Inland Revenue 64p—making the subscription worth nearly two thirds as much again as one which is *not* paid under covenant.

Two Thirds

Perhaps what puts people off covenanting is that they have to commit themselves to pay a subscription for at least seven years. But some 85 per cent of our members renew their subscriptions each year anyway, so there cannot be many for whom this is a deterrent.

Is there a lot of paper work? No—not for the member, though there is quite a bit for us. There is a form to be filled in when you make the covenant in the first place. It is part of the ordinary membership form and the only possible complication is that your signature must be witnessed. The covenant form (or deed of covenant to give its proper title) states that the member will pay annually 'such a sum as, after deduction of income tax at the standard rate for the time being in force, amounts to £............ (this is the net amount you will have to pay each year)'. This means that if you are paying the normal £1 subscription you fill in the figure '1' where the dots are.

After that there is one form a year (R.185) issued by the Inland Revenue.

─────────────────
**Wally Smith is Hon. Treasurer of the R.A.*

This is called the Certificate of Deduction of Income Tax. It certifies that the member actually has paid the tax which the R.A. is going to claim back. This form is sent by Head Office to each covenanting member annually as long as the covenant lasts. Most of it has already been filled up when the member gets it. All he has to do is sign it and write in his business address, or the name of his employer or, if he has neither, his private address. We supply a stamped and addressed envelope for posting the form back to the office.

Declaration

The only other paper work is to add a declaration of the covenant on your or- dinary income tax assessment form. The amount filled in should be the sub- scription plus the income tax benefit going to the R.A. On a £1 subscription for a mem- ber paying tax at the standard rate that means £1.64.

You can of course covenant for any amount more than £1 per annum. Many members already pay sums additional to the basic membership subscription, indicating that they want the extra to go to the Countryside Fund or to the Association's general funds.

There is a small complication, in principle, for those who pay tax at the standard rate *and* whose income is entirely earned in- come. Their effective rate of tax is only seven-ninths of the standard rate and the Inland Revenue *could* claim back from them the difference between the 64p paid to the R.A. and the tax they actually paid. But on a normal subscription this difference is quite negligible and it is unlikely that the Inland Revenue would bother to ask for it.

If You Pay No Tax

Also the scheme does not apply to those who pay no tax, since there is in their case nothing for the Inland Revenue to pay back to the R.A.

With the next issue of *Rucksack* we shall be sending you your membership form. This time, why not open it up and fill in the deed of covenant?

It will cost you a couple of minutes and about the same amount of time each year thereafter. It will be worth a great deal more to the R.A.

Appendix G
Model of handbill for rally   *(front)*

SAVE BEACON HILL

Beacon Hill—one of the loveliest remaining stretches of Chiltern downland—is still threatened by the M40. The Ministry of Transport have not yet withdrawn their proposal for a road in a 150 ft deep cutting alongside the hill.

But there is a perfectly viable alternative put forward by objectors at the public inquiry last year. And there is a new Minister of Transport whose attitude is as yet unknown—so the next few weeks are vital.

You can hear the case against the Ministry proposals at an open air meeting on Stokenchurch Common (village centre and under cover if wet) at 2 pm on Saturday 29th August.

Speakers:

GEOFFREY JELLICOE
(past President Institute of Landscape Architects and principal author of the alternative route)

RICHARD FITTER
(writer, naturalist and Chairman of the Berks, Bucks and Oxon Naturalists' Trust)

CHRISTOPHER HALL
(Vice-President Chiltern Society, Secretary of Ramblers' Association and member of national executive of Council for the Protection of Rural England)

Chairman:

TOM STEPHENSON
(President Ramblers' Association, member of Bucks County Council Countryside Committee and Executive member of Friends of the Vale of Aylesbury).

After the meeting there will be a walk-in along public paths from Stokenchurch across the line of the Ministry route.

The meeting and walk-in are jointly organised by the **Chiltern Society,** the **Oxfordshire Branch** of the **Council for the Protection of Rural England** and the **Southern Area of the Ramblers' Association.** The organisers are grateful to Stokenchurch Parish Council for their help and co-operation.

CHILTERN WALK·IN

(back)

M40 Scandal

The Ministry of Transport plan for the M40 is one of the most outrageous cases of official vandalism on record. Any motorway route down the Chiltern escarpment must be damaging to natural beauty. But the Ministry of Transport engineers chose the worst route and successive Ministers have stuck to it despite the fact that a viable and far less damaging alternative has now been found.

The alternative—the so-called Arup-Jellicoe route—was put forward by objectors at the public inquiry last year. The objectors asked that the Minister should fully study and cost this route before deciding the issue.

The last Minister of Transport refused. He said that his route was best for amenity. But who agrees with him? 'Not the Countryside Commission, official advisers to the Government on countryside issues. Not the Nature Conservancy whose Aston Rowant Reserve will be carved up by the Ministry route. Not the Royal Fine Art Commission whose advice on road structures the Ministry often seeks. Not the Minister's own Advisory Committee on the Landscaping of Trunk Roads who have been refused the opportunity to consider the alternative route. And certainly not the thousands of people who enjoy the views from the Christmas Common ridge-top road every summer.

The alternative route would descend the escarpment through the woodland north and east of the existing A40. It would thus be partially screened; its cutting would be shallower than the Ministry's and its interchange with the proposed Lewknor by-pass would be lower and 400 yards further from the village.

Now the arguments are being placed before the new Minister. On Saturday August 29th you can add your argument by coming to the meeting and taking part in the walk-in afterwards. A massive demonstration of public opinion could be the clinching factor.

Stop it Now

**2 p.m. SATURDAY, 29th AUGUST
STOKENCHURCH COMMON**

Appendix H: Division of local government functions

	COUNTIES	DISTRICTS
Consumer protection	Weights and measures, trade descriptions; Explosives, food and drugs.	Markets and fairs; building regulations.
Education	County is the education authority except in metropolitan counties.	Metropolitan districts are education authorities.
Environmental health	Animal diseases; fire precautions in offices, shops and railway premises.	Food safety and hygiene; communicable diseases; slaughter-houses; factories; safety in the home; water and sewerage (subject to general reorganization of water control).
Fire	Fire services are a county responsibility subject to amalgamation schemes.	
Highways	Counties are highway authorities but district councils may claim maintenance powers for footpaths, bridleways and urban roads which are neither trunk nor classified roads. Counties and districts will exercise concurrent powers over pavement lighting, footpaths and bridleway surveys and their signposting. Footpath and bridleway protection: counties and districts will have concurrent powers.	

	COUNTIES	DISTRICTS
Housing		A district function, including provision, management, slum clearance, house and area improvement—subject only to reserve powers at county level.
Libraries	A county function except in metropolitan counties.	A metropolitan district function.
Museums and art galleries	Concurrent powers to be exercised by county and district authorities.	
Personal social services	A county function except in metropolitan counties.	A metropolitan district function.
Planning	Structure plans; development plan schemes (in consultation with districts); national parks.	Local plans (except in national parks) subject to development plan schemes and structure plans; development control (i.e. decisions on individual planning applications); listed building control.

Concurrent powers: derelict land; country parks, conservation areas; building preservation notices; tree preservation; acquisition and disposal of land for planning purposes, development and redevelopment.

	COUNTIES	DISTRICTS
Police	County function, but subject to amalgamation schemes.	
Recreation	Small holdings	Allotments; local licensing.
	Concurrent powers over: swimming-baths, parks and open spaces; physical training and recreation.	
Refuse	Disposal.	Collection.
Transport and Traffic	Transport planning; traffic, parking (but see opposite); road safety.	Off-street parking, subject to county transport plan.
Youth employment	A county function except in metropolitan counties.	A metropolitan district function.

Appendix I
Proof of evidence

**Proof of Evidence of James Henry Bloggs on Behalf of the
East Barsetshire Preservation Society**

Mr Bloggs will say:

1. My name is James Henry Bloggs. I live at 14 The Crescent,
   Barchester. I am an accountant by profession and I serve
   in an honorary capacity as Secretary of the East Barsetshire
   Preservation Society.

2. The aims of the Society, as stated in its constitution, are:
   'To promote the conservation and enhancement of the
   natural beauty of East Barsetshire for the benefit and enjoy-
   ment of all.' The Society has 3,526 members and 138 corporate members, including ten local authorities and 31
   parish councils.

3. I give this evidence pursuant to Minute No. 53/72 of the
   Executive Committee of the Society, which reads: 'Committee considered and debated proposals by the Central
   Electricity Generating Board for the erection of a switching
   station on land known as Hellings Piece, Plumstead.
   Agreed: that the Society enter formal objection to these
   proposals; that the Secretary be instructed to take all necessary steps to secure their rejection by the planning authority
   or, if need be, by the Secretary of State for Trade and Industry.'

4. The proposed switching station will occupy a site of some 13
   acres. The equipment at the station will reach a height of 20
   feet and four transmission lines carried on towers will lead
   to and from it.

5. The site is partly on cultivated agricultural land and partly on an area of rough grazing belonging to the same farm. Two public paths (Plumstead 15 and Plumstead 23) cross the site. The area of rough grazing, though not open to the public *de jure*, has long been used as a picnic site and recreational area without objections from successive occupiers of the land.

6. The site is screened by rising ground from the nearby B 4255 road. The station will, however, be visible from the greater part of the rough grazing area. But the site will be in full view from the summit of Bishop's Hill, which lies about a quarter of a mile away to the west. Bishop's Hill is common land; a public footpath leads to the summit from the car park set up by the East Barset County Council on the road below the hill. The hill is an extremely popular viewpoint.

7. On eight Sundays during last August and September members of this Society counted the totals of persons on the hill at 2.30 and 4.30 pm. I summarize the figures:

	5/8	12/8	19/8	26/8	2/9	9/9	16/9	23/9
2.30	143	43	202	193	81	156	138	142
4.30	192	51	264	241	124	181	187	196
		(rain)						

I shall hand in more detailed figures relating to other days of the week and also to the area at Hellings Piece, which is to be the site of the switching station.

8. The countryside in which the site lies is among the pleasantest in the County. It is purely agricultural and quite unspoiled. It is noted as an area of high landscape value on the County Development Plan.

9. We consider that a structure on the scale proposed by the CEGB and the necessary transmission lines will form a quite alien intrusion into this countryside.

10. We have suggested to the CEGB that the switching station should be sited at Berrows' Waste in the parish of St Ewolds. This site is surrounded on three sides by conifer afforestation of no attraction, and through which rides exist capable of

carrying the transmission lines. On the fourth side is the Barchester Corporation sewage works and an engineering factory.

11. We understand that the CEGB have rejected this alternative on the ground that it will cost an extra £783,000. We dispute this figure and another witness will speak on that point in detail. But, if the figure is accepted as correct, we consider a matter of £3/4 m. a small sum to pay for the preservation of countryside which gives pleasure to many thousands of people every year.

Notes
1. The above is of course much abbreviated. In practice the witness would go into far more detail, especially about the routes and siting of transmission towers.
2. Paragraph 1. This is the usual form. It is customary, not mandatory.
3. Paragraph 3 is vital. It is not necessary to put the resolution in the proof as here, but you must have a proper resolution, and if necessary the organization's minute book or signed minutes to support it. Cross-examining counsel sometimes try to show that the Society has not acted constitutionally.

Appendix J
Civil service career structure

Permanent Secretary   £15,925   ⎫
Deputy Secretary   £10,675   ⎬ the open
Under-Secretary   £8,425   ⎬ structure
Assistant Secretary   £5,525–£7,451 ⎭

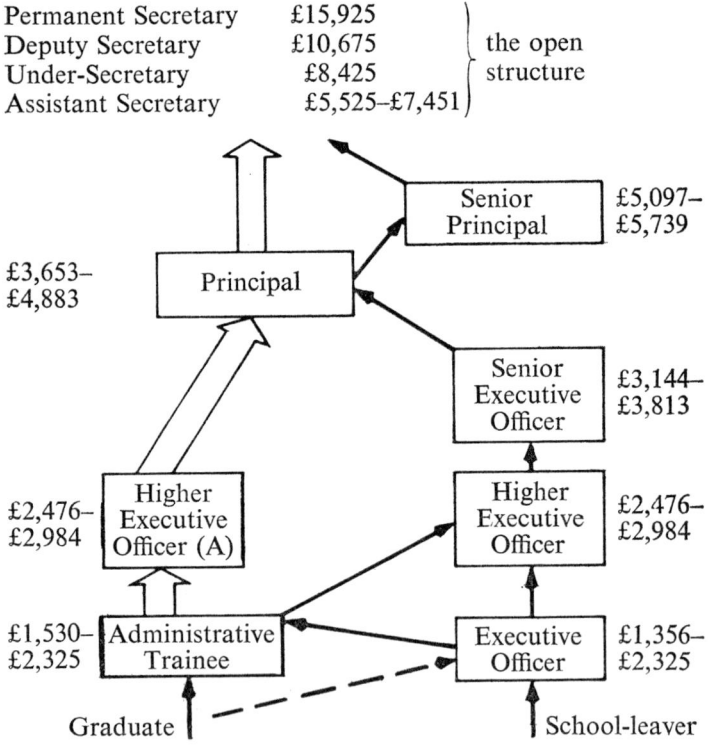

Notes

1 All salaries are those operative for Central London, December 1972.

2 The double arrows mark the fast-stream career.

148

Index

Index